TEACH ME THAT I MAY TEACH . . .

(or what we learned thinking *we* were homeschooling the kids.)

Barbara & Doug Smith

Third Floor Publishing
Post Office Box 827
Arnold, Maryland 21012
410/974-1111

"This hope we have as an anchor of the soul..."
Hebrews 6:19

Printed in the United States of America

ISBN 1-878140-06-X
Third Printing: 1998

GRATEFUL ACKNOWLEDGEMENTS

I've treasured the opportunity to write for the *Arundel Homeschoolers' Newsletter* as much as I've "enjoyed" homeschooling. My articles for the newsletter led to this book. I want to share what I've been learning about the unfailing grace and goodness of God.

I am grateful that my husband Doug kept reading my drafts and encouraging me. I am grateful for the pastors of our church, Glenn Parkinson, Tom Wenger, and Jerry McFarland, who faithfully preach and teach the word of God. Thanks to Walkersville Christian Family Schools for their faithful administration of our home-school, and for their support and prayers; and especially to Ed Rodatus who could see beyond my fixation with commas. Thanks also to Beth Richardson and Suzanne Mulloy who fine-tuned this little effort. We are grateful to Susan Kennerly, a homeschool mom who caught a few bloopers when she read our book. I am grateful also to Cindy and Joe Schell who designed the artwork for our book.

And special thanks to our son and daughter, an inspiration and joy in our lives - without whom there might not have been such priceless lessons. I bless the Lord for both of you!

PREFACE

The following pieces are lessons I have learned homeschooling our son and daughter. My most painful lessons have been the most profitable, and no corner was so dark the Lord didn't light the way out. I hope those who read this will see the goodness of Jesus Christ.

CONTENTS

INTRODUCTION

I once wrote, "During the past few months, at least four women decades younger than I asked me, 'Do you work?' Knowing I *should* stand firm in my chosen profession - homemaking - nevertheless I faltered, hemming and hawing. My gallant husband suggested I answer, "No, I don't work, but I give a good imitation! "

Doug and I hope these "imitations" will brighten and enlighten frazzled homeschooling veterans, or shaky rookies! During a recent sermon, our pastor exhorted us not to waste our suffering, so we are offering our experiences homeschooling to encourage other families to persevere! This collaboration is an accumulation of some penetrating but edifying experiences. We have also included some ruminations about living in the "body" of Christ and some thoughts about the holidays -- sometimes a source of family stress.

Our homeschooling experience is not so different from those who have gone before us; but the lessons we learned have been precious to us. We pray that if our struggles sound familiar, our observations and experiences will gladden your heart and spur you on.

Douglas and I work together in our publishing company and have homeschooled our two children, ages 18 and 14 for eight years. Our son completed his high school requirements and concurrently completed fifty-six hours of classes at the local community college. He attends college now full time. Our daughter is a high school student at home. Both children work in the "family" business.

Doug writes and I edit his books for people claiming Social Security disability benefits and their physicians, through our company *Physicians' Disability Services*. Publications include a guide for physicians who write disability reports, a workbook for claimants to document their disability, and an illustrated disability handbook. Doug is an attorney, a graduate of Georgetown Law School, and I am a graduate of the University of Maryland. I produce a newsletter for homeschoolers, which Doug edits. Now that we have gotten over being personally offended with the other's comments, we work pretty well together!

Barbara Smith

PART ONE

Character Training:
Theirs

"Children be obedient to your parents in all things, for this is well-pleasing to the Lord." **Colossians 3:20**

Teach Me Lord, That I May Teach

Change happens daily, whether you see it or not! When I thumb through our family's photo albums, the record of how our angelic, bright-eyed darlings changed into the marvelous people they are now, bewilders me. Why didn't I notice the change? I remember wondering when they were small, whether I had been caught in a time-warp of busy little hands, cartoons and characters from Sesame Street. During that time, a tiny gnawing in my heart, a fear, took root. Would the drudgery of wiping pudgy fingers, spills and spatters, ever produce anything but more of the same tedious routine? I never grasped that daily, all our lives were consistently changing, while appearing to stay the same.

Training Occurs Daily, Whether You Intend It or Not!
As surely and subtly as our children grew, so we taught many *unintended* lessons. We had no conception of the limits of our "classroom." Teaching children is not a privilege of certified classroom teachers. It is the principal charge that the Lord gives to parents, and is as important as feeding, clothing and sheltering our young.

Children learn as much from our examples as they do from our words, figuring out quickly what's important by OUR response. Like scanners, their little eyes and hearts pick up our attitudes quickly, though perhaps they always don't "read" them correctly.

Children can quickly find out our frame of mind by watching what we do, and how we do it. Wishing for something more interesting or challenging to do when the laundry and dishes pile up is easy to identify - especially if we sigh loud enough!

Teaching children doesn't mean training them to be obedient little robots. Training our children means we must first introduce them to the Lord. If they haven't made His acquaintance, how can they learn His lessons? Training children is giving them the skills they need to grow up spiritually as well as physically and emotionally. Effective parenting does not require a degree, but it does require prayer, thought, resolve and the one ingredient none of us ever has enough of . . . time.

Quality Time vs. Quantity Time
Your time is a very precious commodity, and while you may want to guard your treasure, the reality is that instilling discipline in children takes time. Learning what the Lord teaches does take time. Pausing to think about how to discipline (not condemn) for infractions takes time - lots of time, lots of completely engaged and focused time.

"Doing things *right* takes time." Isn't that what *your* Mom told you? AAGGHHH!!! Where will the hours come from? They will come probably from your hoard of "personal" time.

"Is it wise to spend so much time training my kids now?" you ask. "Shouldn't we wait until we can reason with the children?" Waiting is a luxury. The stages that winsome, willful toddler is currently passing through may be a rehearsal of longer-running, but less engaging performances to come. Consider the time you spend training now as an investment opportunity you may not have in later years.

The body of Christ is blessed because many faithful parents took time to train their children. Many strong servants of the Lord such as John Newton, Adoniram Judson, George Mueller, and Elizabeth Prentiss had moms who prayed and obeyed the Lord, especially through dark days. How much time are you willing to devote to training your children?

Timely, Thoughtful and Practical Parenting
Christian parents know our children's heavenly Creator, therefore we can pray for insight, obey what we know, and humbly ask for continued guidance. We can keep to our task of prayer and obedience. He has promised to keep to His tasks. Today is an ideal time to begin training our children; not tomorrow. (If you worry that you waited too long to start reining your kids, START NOW! The Lord is an excellent coach for playing "catch-up.")

What do you need? Persistence, a sense of humor AND a sense of timing are essential for raising children. Keep your goals simple, and be certain your training goals are the Lord's goals. We aren't training "good kids" to look good ourselves. We should be steadfast, conscientious stewards of what the Lord has given us, even when the "rewards" may not be obvious.

Don't be surprised or disappointed if your children resist training. "Where," you ask, "does my child get such a will to ignore my instructions?" Well, where did you get yours? Self-will is not a pretty thing to behold. Shaping the will, while not breaking the spirit, is a spiritual battle. Some things only come out by prayer and fasting. Put aside whatever is hindering your fellowship with God, pray and persist.

Don't assume that you are failing when the crown prince and princess continue to reject your authority. He created that precious child who is confounding you and exhausting your strength, and He perfectly planned *you* to be the very parent to bring up this child! He did not make a mistake. When you and an heir lock horns, in the midst of the battle recognize that the Lord Himself is your unfailing helper.

**Design, Describe & Discipline -
Or Write Your Own Child Rearing Manual!**
Don't begin to rein in your children until you and the Lord have reached agreement on what your training goals are. Seek His counsel first. Make certain both parents agree on the family ground rules and the method of discipline. Clearly express to your children what you expect and why you expect it. Carefully explain the "House Rules" keeping particulars simple. Describe how you intend to enforce infractions, *and stick to it.*

Becky Wyand, a wise mom, teacher, and education specialist for Walkersville Christian Family Schools, suggests keeping a record of your prayers for your child. Take time now to observe and record your children's strengths and struggles. Be precise and pray with an open Bible, seeking the Lord's answers. The Book of Proverbs is filled with possibilities for a parent's prayers.

After Observation - Action!
Children, our own precious bundles included, don't simply outgrow the temptation to defy authority. They merely refine their technique, unless they are given a reason to submit. If you observe a violation of the "Rules," discipline promptly. Even if you can do no more now than remind them you will address the infraction when you return to the privacy of your home, do it firmly! The point of discipline is to teach our children they are not a law unto themselves; there is a higher authority whom they must obey - and to whom the

parents must also submit!

Never overlook your contribution to your child's misbehavior. Reexamine your own conduct if you believe your child is controlling you instead of obeying you.

- Is God real to you?
- Did you fail to establish meaningful guidelines and expectations?
- Did you fail to explain the "rules" and the consequences?
- Did you fail to follow through on discipline?
- Did you react in exasperation and anger, instead of quiet and calm persistence?
- Did your child express a need, which you ignored, because you had other plans?

We're Still at It, Too.

We parents continue training our children until the Lord calls us home. We set examples and standards by our attitudes and actions, until our last breath. However the tools of discipline pass from our hands. Our children will soon enough begin to experience "discipline" by tools held in less loving hands than their parents. Teach them to accept their heavenly Father's supervision and protection.

The days of Sesame Street, Mr. Rogers, and Fisher-Price have faded so swiftly that I would relish a trip back in time to enjoy my little boy and girl. However, "backward" isn't the proper direction. All those indistinguishable changes which later become so clear from photos in the albums, have culminated in soon to be independent *grown* children. This will happen for your family also. One morning you will see across the breakfast table from you a young man or young woman eager to live life as the person they've become.

15

So, from my bag of "If I'd only's" may I exhort you? Don't be blown around by every fashionable wind, figure out a regime, and stick to it unless the Lord changes it. He wanted you to raise the very children He gave you. He promised never to leave or forsake you, and He is not going to abandon us after entrusting *His* children to our care! We must take time and give time, and in time there will be a harvest pleasing to the Lord, for *He* will do it.

Do Your Pupils Know What You Know?

The Baltimore *Sun* reported in February of 1994
that none of the 17 Anne Arundel county middle schools
met the 1993 Maryland School Performance Assessment
Standards. The tests are designed to show how well the
students can apply their knowledge and how well the
schools are delivering the skills the students will need in
the next century. Also, more than one half of the 76
elementary schools failed to meet those skill levels.
Homeschoolers are exempt from most standardized test
rituals, but do you ever wonder how well our children
can apply their knowledge; are homeschooling parents
passing on "skills" our children will need in the next
century?

If Homeschooling Were Not an Option . . .
The flurry of activities and the roller coaster of emotions
involved with responding to the federal bill HR-6 (that
might have paralyzed homeschooling) left me numb and
exhausted. Nervous that the "certification" might knock
all of us out of the homeschooling nest, I began to
wonder how well have we trained our children if we
were confronted with returning them to a traditional
school.

Initially we chose to homeschool for academic
reasons, pursuing a better strategy to guide our
children's education. I had visions of the kids qualifying
for Harvard - perhaps as brain surgeons - all because of
homeschooling. Later, we realized academic proficiency
was secondary to character training.

Gradually, we realized our education goals should
not be limited to spawning children who fit the world's

definition of "educated." Our education goals must first qualify them as godly men or women. "PhD's" are worthy goals, but as Jim Elliot suggested, "AuG's" are more important, for those who win them are *Approved unto God.* The apostle Paul described the hope beneath our homeschooling: *"Be diligent to present yourself approved to God as a workman who does not need to be ashamed, handling accurately the word of truth."* 2 Timothy 2:15 How will our children learn this, though, without a teacher?

A Teacher Who Taught His Student Well
A recent sermon on "suffering for righteousness" fixed my attention on the extent a teacher can influence his or her students. The sermon began and ended with mention of Polycarp, an early martyr at the hands of the Romans. Elderly, but vibrant, he died bravely and with great dignity in atrocious circumstances.

Did you know that Polycarp was closely linked to John, the disciple whom Christ loved? The apostle John listened to Jesus and in turn taught Polycarp. Polycarp not only endured to the end, but triumphed. Seeing that connection reinforced the urgent purpose of teaching our children. More than enduring, I pray our children will *triumph*!

Preparedness for life is the core value of all educators, but especially of Christian parents. Unfortunately, our priorities get all tangled up, however innocently, with the world's agenda for the children. Christ knew the perils His disciples faced and prepared them. In turn, they may have been disappointed that Christ did not immediately return, but they prepared those in their care to live while the Church waited for the Savior's return.

18

Are You Reflecting or Generating Light?

How are we presenting our home education program? Do we see it as something to get through to lay hold of one of the world's prizes? Or is our educational plan for our children something to savor, because we are offering the substance from which spiritual and intellectual muscle is made?

Can our kids soar if the nest *is* upset? They will leave the nest, some sooner than others, to face a world that hates God. Their "soaring" skills will be greatly influenced by how they see their parents "fly."

The First Cause of Education: Character Training

Character training takes place every moment of everyone's day, in peaceful moments or stress-filled ones (Romans 5:3-5). The crises that threaten to undo us both shape and reveal our character and our trust in God. Do our kids see their parents' prayerful dependence on God? Do they see their diligent study of His word, that is equal to or greater than their dependence on the world's wisdom? How does your devotional time compare with the time you spend perusing the newspapers?

Our children are moving into a world that appears no longer to value the Christian religion, even culturally. Worse, the Church seems befuddled about its responsibilities. Are the children learning to apply their knowledge, standing on a sure foundation of the Word of God, because you, their teacher, taught them, and modeled how to do it?

To whom are *you* listening, teacher and what are *you* teaching? The apostle John listened to Jesus, and in turn taught Polycarp. Polycarp not only endured to the end, but triumphed!

19

Built Any Altars Lately?

"Perhaps my sons have sinned and cursed God in their hearts. " Job 1:5

How often do you pray for your children? What do you pray for them? What dangers to your children's well-being drive you to your knees? How dangerous do you believe the sin is that so easily entangles and entraps our children and us?

Centuries ago, a blameless, upright father of seven sons and three daughters left a legacy of prayer and sacrifice for his children as an answer to these questions. His prayers for his children's spiritual well-being were one gift of eternal value he gave them, for they did not live to inherit his earthly treasures.

Though he was a man of property and wealth and a man who feared God and turned from evil, Job rose, as a servant would, early in the morning and offered burnt offerings continually according to the number of his children. For Job said, "Perhaps my sons have sinned and cursed God in their hearts." Job 1:15

Did Job Have Bad Kids?

In Scripture, Job's children were numbered *before* his possessions, and described immediately *after* his relationship to God. Though adults living apart from Job, they undoubtedly knew their father's righteousness and his continual sacrificial offerings and prayers on their behalf. Why did this ancient father ceaselessly entreat the

Lord's forgiveness for the possibility of secret sin when his family's lives seemed serene?

Job rightly feared God. Therefore, even the notion that one of his dear children may have sinned, cursing God in his or her heart, kindled his prayers. Burnt offerings were costly and time-consuming, even for rich men like Job. Yet the father offered his sacrifice of property and time before the Lord continually. *Have your prayers for your children equaled even a fraction of what Job invested in his children?*

Where is Your Prayer Emphasis?

We invest time in our children to be sure. What is the goal of our investment? We fervently train our children to avoid external snares, but do we pray as fervently for them to revere God? To be holy because God is holy? Do you fear God more than you fear the decay and decline of our world? Do your children know this?

When our adorable babies grow into walking, thinking, talking persons, we see the limitation of external controls to corral determined offspring. As they mature into the young men and women, our children thrill us with their accomplishments and humble us with their gifts and talents. Yet, sadly, our beloved children distress us when they stumble, and we, like Job, long to intercede before the Lord for their hearts' purity. *How can we pray for their hearts?*

Matthew Henry, commenting in the seventeenth century on Job, suggests a path. Though parents cannot give grace to our children (it is God that sanctifies), we can emulate Job who like Abraham had an altar for his family and *rose early as one whose heart was upon his work*. We can, like Job, bless our children, laying each

21

on the altar, and ask God to give each a pure heart and a clear conscience.

Do your children know you pray for them? Would they count you as their prayer warrior? Do they know what your prayers are for them? Do they know their well-being is so important to you, that you will take time to speak to the Lord on their behalf?

Don't Wait to Give Them Their Inheritance!
Christ, the perfect sin offering, invites us to the altar of prayer to sacrifice that elusive and costly commodity - TIME in prayer for the children He has given us. Whatever their age and stage, ask now that each child would be receptive to the Holy Spirit's conviction of sin. Continually ask that each child's conscience (and our own!) would be open to the Holy Spirit who impresses upon each the desire to repent, and gives grace to be holy.

Lonely?

"A man of many friends comes to ruin, but there is a friend who sticks closer than a brother." Proverbs 18:24

"My child seems lonely," many homeschooling parents fret. "Will our child's loneliness influence his ability to learn?" we ask. Critics of homeschooling are quick to argue that the lack of peer interaction may have dire consequences for homeschooled students. They say children may not be learning important lessons about dealing with peers of other backgrounds.* "Part of life is growing up with your peers ... learning for instance, to compete and debate," said Harry D. Shapiro, a Baltimore lawyer and member of the State Board of Education. ** Homeschooling parents may begin to wonder if a traditional classroom environment would be a better vehicle than schooling at home to alleviate loneliness, especially in older children. Where can we find the solution to this predicament?

Students in a classroom of 25-30 seldom complain of *loneliness*. They complain about homework, or cliques, about boredom, the food or about gym - but the crush of bodies camouflages the feelings of loneliness. At

---

* Anastasia Walsh, "Popularity of home schools worries critics," *The (Annapolis, Maryland) Capital,* December 19, 1994.

** Ibid.

home, however, free from many peculiarities of "peer" schooling, our children may become painfully aware of a conspicuous fact of the human condition: loneliness.

Loneliness is an emotional response; so is anger, fear, joy, and sadness. Each passes, usually as the circumstances change. When our beloved children explode in anger, or whimper with fear, our first response is not to put them in a new learning environment, or introduce a new set of pals! No, we admonish them; we pray and encourage them to pray!

What is the Point of Loneliness?
Rushing to fill voids with extra sports activities, friends, diversions and entertainment, we might miss an important opportunity. A child's sense of loneliness is an opportunity for both parent and child to draw close to our heavenly Father, asking Him what the remedy is for our loneliness. Searching to deliver our children from what society defines as a *difficulty* in educating children at home, we may unwittingly give up a powerful spiritual object lesson.

Get your Bibles out and together ask God, "Why are we lonely? Who cares? Why do we want friends? Who created friendships? Why are friendships important to God?"

Unfortunately, pursuing the Lord may be the last step parents take to encourage our "lonely" children. Yet throughout Scripture we can read of those who cry out in lonely anguish to God. *"I lie awake, I have become like a lonely bird on a housetop."* Psalm 102:7

From Lamentations 1:1, we discover that desolation, "aloneness," may be an unhappy circumstance, but it is not a bad vantage point for spiritual insight. How can we pray, if we don't see a need?

An afflicted man cries out ... *"Hear my prayer O lord, and let my cry for help come to Thee"* Psalm 102:1.

Loneliness *is* the condition of the human heart, especially the heart wandering from its Creator and best friend. If our kids are restless at home, do they reflect our own restlessness ... A conviction that something better lies beyond the doors of our home ... friends, adventure, stimulation, pleasure? Do we model for our children "contentment" as we wait for answers to prayers? Is the Lord any less interested in your child's emotional well-being than He is in their education? What does God want? Finding good companionship, and becoming a good companion is something our children can pray about.

The Lord gives the lonely an oasis. *"God makes a home for the lonely; he leads out the prisoners into prosperity; only the rebellious live in a parched land."* (Psalm 68:6) Do you see your home as a sanctuary, created by God to refresh and nourish LONELY people? Have we become friends with our family, so we can teach our children the value of the relationships God has provided?

The Gift of Friendship

Randomly plopping our children into a passel of peers, be they neighbor children, church friends, teammates, or even other home schoolers, may not be the prescription for alleviating loneliness. Parents remembering many of their own experiences may conclude that indiscriminate immersion in a variety of social groups and activities doesn't wipe out loneliness or guarantee satisfying friendships.

Friendship and fellowship are indeed sweet and intimate ingredients of a vibrant spiritual and social life. While their absence will intensify the emotion of loneliness, does their scarcity make us any less useful to God? Have we told our children this? Lonely people have been used greatly by God . . . Abraham, Naomi, Ruth, Samson, all knew great times of aloneness.

Remember David? David longed for the sweetness of friendship and experienced for a season a friendship that was more precious to him than the love of a woman (2 Samuel 1:26). After Jonathan died, David never again knew the blessing of an intimate friend. Still we remember David as the Lord described him, "a man after His own heart," if not the most popular in the senior class. Are we preparing our children to be the friend Jonathan was for David, as well as praying that they will gain a companion like Jonathan?

Remember Lot? Lot longed for the world, and chose to live where the action was. His wife and his daughters learned well what their peers believed important! Lot must have had many lonely hours to reflect upon the training he provided his children. (Genesis 19)

Parents must be wise as we assess our children's needs. If our children are continually friendless, we must consider what we are teaching and why. If we are restricting our children too much from being with friends, we should prayerfully examine this issue. However, simply injecting them into a group won't necessarily solve the problem of loneliness. Immersing our kids in a crowd of interesting, busy peers may divert a young person ... but from what, to what?

How to respond to loneliness and how to choose friends and diversions are subjects we can address candidly in home education. And God is *the* expert on these subjects. Can God meet the needs of a "lonely" child, you wonder. Have you asked Him?

Sailing Through Homeschooling

"Oh, that they had such a heart in them, that they would fear Me, and keep all my commandments always, that it may be well with them and with their sons forever."
Deuteronomy 5:29

The image of sailboats gliding effortlessly across the Chesapeake Bay is a pleasant Maryland memory for most of us. However those of us who have sailed the Bay know the weather is never completely "pacific." Sudden squalls and shoal water have wrecked more than one outing! Yes, sailing the Chesapeake is an apt metaphor to our homeschooling "voyage."

Are you sailing on course or are squalls blowing you off-course? Is your homeschooling vessel drifting into shoal water, in danger of running aground?
If getting through the books is our objective, then simply finishing our "school" work is enough. However what was God's aim in giving us children to raise? The Lord commands parents to train their children in the fear and admonition of Himself, for a child's well-being depends upon it. *"... For the commandment is a lamp, and the teaching is light; and reproofs for discipline are the way of life ..."* Proverbs 6:23; see also Proverbs 7:2 and Ecclesiastes 12.

Are you content with the academic progress? Are you completing texts, projects and papers, while conquering math and spelling facts? Good! How's the character training at your house? Too many characters, and too little training?

Seriously, do your children listen to your instruction? Are they finding wisdom? Are they gaining understanding?

Are you?

Or, are you becoming desperate because your children *never* obey without an argument, a sigh or a comment? A child's attitude, words, facial expressions or body language frequently reveal a defiant spirit. Even that sweet baby toddling about your kitchen is trying to chart her own course. Attitudes are as contagious as colds.

A recalcitrant spirit in one child disrupts the day's lessons, and then sweeps through the other children, infecting them. Then, despite the planning, your most creative lessons fizzle because your toddler distracts your older kids. Field trips or special instruction is spoiled because of squabbling siblings. Suddenly, you hear yourself begging, then threatening your children to complete assignments. Even devotions and Bible study become a battlefield!

Consistent character training in the midst of phonics, fractions, and photosynthesis -- while keeping house -- is tough. Also, the fruit of consistent character training is not instantaneous. Character training includes conflict and delays!

This ongoing struggle can take the wind from the most committed home-schooling sails. In fact, your schooling may be foundering because of these time-consuming clashes. Are the clashes blowing you off course? Seasoned sailors will testify that wandering a degree or two off course means missing the mark by many miles.

Let me post a storm warning. If you are clinging to the hope that your little rebels will simply outgrow their foolishness, beware! What they learn to get away with now may well become the habits of their lives. *"But a child who gets his own way brings shame to his mother."* Proverbs 29:15b. If you have charted a course of character training, secured to the word of the Master, remain at the helm. Our children risk eternal separation from God if we slough off our office to teach them the fear of the Lord (Proverbs 1:28-31).

Fortunately, the Lord Jesus is our constant sailing master, our sure guide, even for algebra and grammar, but especially for character training (See Deuteronomy 31:6). Do you believe this? Christ knows the best program for each child's intellectual and physical development. He shows us, through Bible study, prayer, research and waiting. So too, He leads us to train our children as they mature spiritually.

How? First, He instructs *us*. Ask yourself, is His word my lamp; do I fear Him and keep His commands? Our kids are quick to spot hypocrisy, for they have spent their entire lives observing us! Before we produce godly children, we must be godly parents. We can't demand from our children what we have been negligent to practice. Because the Lord is orderly, our carelessness, disorganization or haphazard approaches to homemaking and child rearing responsibilities don't bring honor to Him.

Second, He commands us to tell our children what He has done for us (Deuteronomy 11). Start today! *Now* is the time to rein in that unruly toddler or willful preschooler with prayer, the Word of God and consistent training. If you can't manage your toddlers, ask Christ to intercede!

How will you handle the sixteen year old who towers over you if you can't cope with a pint-sized insurgent? *Now* is the time to renew fervently your prayers and petitions for your older children. Wishing things would be better, doesn't make them so! Never rely upon a wishbone when a backbone is required.

Don't put off instructing even your youngest children to fear the Lord, and revere His Word; don't give up training your oldest. No child ever grows beyond needing his or her parents' prayers. Even if the spiritual training has been a hopeless muddle until this very moment, ask Christ to intercede!

Make the time to study the Bible, pray and wait upon Christ. For this is the underpinning of our parenting and homeschooling. How we teach what we believe is a mighty lesson; how we live is a mightier one.

Would Your Kids Go West With *You*?

*"I know that Thou canst do all things and that no
purpose of thine can be thwarted."* Job 42:2

Pioneers who traveled west were a curious bunch
who made a profound impression on America. Historian
Frederick Jackson Turner, who lived from 1861 to 1932,
wrote that emigrating Americans both moved a boundary
and formed a national character as they pushed the
frontier from Appalachia to the Pacific Ocean. Those
who rode with their children in covered wagons (the
"Conestoga" or later in "prairie schooners") set quite a
standard. They endured disease, deprivation,
disappointment and sometimes death because they
believed with all their hearts a better life lay somewhere
in the west. The parents risked everything to secure a
better future for themselves and their kids.

Homeschooling families are also a curious bunch.
Many parents testify their adventure can seem as lonely
as a pioneer's journey and many days feel like a wagon
trip across the Dakota "Badlands." However, we believe
like the pioneers that the risk is acceptable because better
educational opportunities for our children exist away
from the established order. Aren't you risking something
to homeschool?

Although they were determined, the pioneers were
wise enough to trust a man, the wagon master, to get

them to their destination. The wagon master's job was to move a diverse band of people safely across inhospitable territory. He built up leaders from among the travelers, provoked the timid to persevere, and disciplined the unruly members. The wagon master had to enforce order, exact compliance and boost endurance. The lives of the pioneers depended upon his experience and his ability, as much as upon their own strength, health and will.

Like our enterprising ancestors, we outfit our home prairie schooner and often band with other daring souls in support groups, becoming a family within a group. Like the pioneers, Christian homeschooling families sign on under a Master, Jesus Christ, who will see us through the desert and over the mountainous obstacles of home education to our destination. He, too, is looking to build leadership, encourage the timid and discipline the unruly so we reach His goals. He is no less demanding than the wagon masters, but He also gives us the capacity -- the heart and strength -- to comply with His demands. Are you following His lead and drawing on His strength?

Traveling west taught members of the wagon train much more than geography. Similarly, homeschooling teaches everybody more than academic facts. Like the trek west, our adventure teaches us who we are and whom we trust. The journey reveals and shapes our characters. Character defines a man or woman, a girl or boy, whether moving from coast to coast, or from subject to subject. Is homeschooling conforming our children to the character of Christ? (Romans 5:1-5).

Like the young people who went west with their parents, our children must depend not only upon our savvy, but on the savvy of our Master to cross safely over hostile ground. Huddled behind us, much the way pioneer kids may have huddled during the long, dark prairie nights, our children are watching. They see who or what is the object of our faith; even little ones listen and watch. They watch our reactions to the daily onslaughts of life's challenges and learn.

How are we building confidence in our children that God is in control? How is homeschooling helping to shape our children's trust in the sovereign will of God? Do we encourage them to "trust in the Lord" while we rely upon the world's ways?

Well-meaning homeschooling parents can focus so intently on describing what is wrong in our culture, we may fail to communicate the power of God in and over any nation. Criticizing and complaining about the stresses, we can tear down our children's confidence in our Master. Sadly, we may be so distracted by worries we neglect our duty to our children (Luke 10: 41,42).

Does our obedience to Christ convince our children that we believe He is the best Master; that we believe God is sufficient for the circumstances of our lives, including our homeschool journey?

Throughout the 1800s' the promise of freedom, land and gold enticed many folks to pull up stakes and head West. For them, surviving and arriving was an achievement, but their arrival was only the beginning of a new venture in the unsettled wilderness. Though many were eccentric, the pioneers' grit and gumption even in the face of failures and heartbreaks, taught their children lessons that shaped the character of generations of Americans. Pioneer children built this nation on the foundations laid by their parents who risked everything for dreams and ambitions and beliefs. Their legacy continues to inspire Americans.

Issues of the quality of education, our children's physical safety, and "values" prompted hundreds of thousands of parents, many of whom are Christian, to pull their children out of mainstream education and to teach their children at home. Getting our children educated will be a tremendous accomplishment, but graduation is only the beginning. When we arrive at our education destination, our kids will not be settling down in the culture, but will be beginning a new journey, wherever Christ calls them to serve . . . and we will too.

Are we teaching them that graduation is not an endpoint? Are we teaching them to learn from the triumphs and the failures, judging nothing by appearances, but testing by the plumb line of Scripture? Will they be able to stand on the foundation we are laying? What will our legacy inspire? Teaching our children to trust the Master who always brings them through, is the best "education" we can give them!

Happy Trails!

The Curriculum Safari - Don't Hunt For What You Already Have!

"His divine power has granted us everything pertaining to life and godliness ... " 2 Peter 1:3

Ah, spring! The time for homeschoolers to begin to stalk the best books, tapes and games to make next year's schooling richer, better, more interesting, and easier on Mom. Nothing excites homeschoolers like the whiff of a popular curriculum fair close-by or a colossal used book sale appearing in our sights.

Honestly now, at recent curriculum fairs didn't you hope to find *the* arithmetic textbook that would teach your "mathematically-challenged" children? Weren't *some* among us searching for a dynamite program to ignite a curiosity in history and geography in our "video dependent" kids; something that won't look like a textbook? Weren't you hoping to find user-friendly material to prime your profoundly uninterested students in English grammar and literature? Come on now, 'fess up. Who doesn't long for an instructional series that could teach physics, for example, *by osmosis?*

Homeschoolers are perpetual explorers. We look for practical but imaginative resources to teach our children to compete in a technologically advanced society. Several incentives spur our explorations. Some at-home educators constantly hunt curricula that will fill the gaps they perceive in their own education. Many parents fret their current home education program doesn't encompass all the pertinent grade-level material for the assorted grades at home. To be blunt, some of us are such unrelenting seekers because we have a nagging misgiving we may not be providing all we should to educate our children.

What Worries You Most?
How much does *fear* drive your curriculum design? We fret that homeschooling might not give our kids what they need to be prepared for life, but do we worry whether homeschooling prepares them for life *after* life? Which is your greater fear: that your child will miss a well-paying fulfilling career, or that the Lord will ignore them?

Should we chuck the books then? No, of course not; we must encourage our children to honor Christ in all their studies and activities -- especially the subjects that are a stretch. And we must be the best teachers *we* can be. As ambassadors for Jesus Christ we are more effective when we are thoughtful and well-informed (2 Corinthians 5:20). So learning is a *good* thing. However, what is the objective?

God warned Israel, an advanced civilization in the ancient world, that His people would be destroyed from *lack* of knowledge. Tragically, because they rejected knowledge, God rejected them and He also *ignored* their children! (Hosea 4:6) What good does "scholarship" do if our children miss the knowledge of their Creator and Redeemer? (Isaiah 44:24-25, Matthew 16:26)

Remember Where the Best Hunting Is!
If you still long to find the comprehensive curriculum, you may need to redirect your exploration. Be sure you are training your children in the fear and admonition of the Lord. (Matthew 6:33) Where can we find an uncom-

plicated method that is doctrinally sound, easily taught and readily understandable?

Look on your bookshelf. The book with embossed gold letters is useful. Or how about the study version, by the same Author, that is three shelves down, crisp and clean in its original dust jacket? Though it has remained unopened, it is chock-full of cross references, study guides, maps and charts. Or maybe you could start with the children's edition under somebody's bed; you know, the one with the charming illustrations of Jesus. No matter how many translations or editions of the Bible you have, begin reading one - today! Begin with Psalm 119. Our children learn best by our examples, when they are watching what you love to study.

God has given us *everything* we need for life and godliness in His Word. Go to Him frequently, willing to be taught, so you can teach. If you want a godly character, and are serious about instructing your children in what pleases God, He will surely guide you to select appropriate academic pursuits and the materials to succeed in them! Don't let this summer melt into autumn without hunting for God's direction for you and your children's education.

He has given His Word so we might know Him. God has given His Holy Spirit to help us learn of His son Jesus Christ. We can get to know Him by opening it regularly and asking for wisdom. (James 1:5) Appraise, please, the following "curriculum planning guides" to take on any education safari . . . and let others know how you bagged the big "catch."

"Curriculum Planning Guides"
Read 2 Peter 1:3-9. Consider memorizing it! How does the promise of being a partaker in His divine nature, and

escaping the corruption that is in the world by lust appeal to you? How does becoming fruitful and effective in your knowledge of our Lord Jesus Christ sound to you? Following Peter's principles, what will you lack when the next academic year begins?

Meditate upon Psalm 119 throughout all your curriculum selection and lesson planning. Ask God to make you mean what Psalm 119 says. Write down what He teaches you . . . learn so you can teach your children.

Pray for your family and personalize 2 Peter 1:3-9 for each of one, and record your prayers. You will see some amazing answers throughout the new academic year!

PART TWO

Character Training:
Mine

"If then you have been raised up with Christ, keep seeking the things above, where Christ is, seated at the right hand of God. Set your mind on the things above, and not on the things that are on earth." **Colossians 3: 1, 2**

Well-Watered Garden

"And the Lord will continually guide you, and satisfy your desire in scorched places, and give strength to your bones; and you will be like a well-watered garden, and like a spring of water whose waters do not fail...
You will be called the repairer of the breach ... "
Isaiah 58:11,12

By the end of school this past spring I was not only *scorched* like a drought damaged garden, but a few of my walls were assuredly breached! Therefore, with the prospect of lazy summer days ahead, I decided to take some advice from Isaiah (chapter 58). I wanted to become like a well-watered garden. Freed from schooling "schedules" I aimed to spend it with the Lord. This summer I intended to prepare a fall harvest of productive "fruit" to sustain a new academic year.

In previous summers I've realized, often too late, that haphazard devotionals leave unsightly gaps in my spiritual "garden," much the way careless gardening spoils the flower beds. Activities that seemed perfect for the lazy warm days of summers past choked off meeting regularly with the Lord - until my life became like a bedraggled garden, overgrown with weeds.

The Lord was faithful; His patience helped me plant some good habits this summer to meet regularly with Him, and I thrived! By spending time in the garden with the Gardener, I saw Him working in my heart to bring forth fruit. For me, spending time with God has

41

been a time of refreshment and renewal, and has increased my thirst for consistent worship and quiet time.

A bountiful garden never sprang full-bloom into being; it began with small fragile plants and grew with cultivation. A lush, mature garden means *someone* invested labor and love and time, even *off-season*. So, too, our spiritual gardens depend upon effort, throughout the seasons. No praiseworthy garden ever sprouted fully mature, able to bloom without cultivation. So, too, our spiritual gardens pass through "seasons" just as our backyard gardens grow, wither and revive again.

Perhaps our intangible gardening seasons are better labeled as anticipation, joy, sorrow and submission, instead of summer, fall, winter, and spring. Some seasons we balk at tending our gardens, like amateur gardeners who balk at weeding, the heat, or insects. Whatever the season, though, no gardener lets the bounty simply languish on the vine - he harvests and uses the produce! Neither does the Lord intend to create ornamental gardens in His people. Isaiah urges those who long to be productive to get busy and use what the Lord is growing to bless those who have not!

Were you overtaken by the busyness of summer? Are you wondering how you will meet the challenge of another academic year? *Go to the garden!* Meet now with God - before the harvest - and spend time with the Lord. "Autumn" gardens can be as productive and pleasing as those planted months before! He is waiting, and He is working. If a well-watered garden can produce a gorgeous, fertile harvest, how much more fruit will your well-watered spiritual garden produce?

Other Handy Gardening Tools: Psalm 23, 90; Isaiah 55.

Changing the Closets

Does anyone out there make a big deal of "switching closets" when the summer slides into autumn? It always takes me forever to sort through my clothes ... Something always seems to gum up the works in process. Or if I do get clothes closets switched promptly, we always have a week of "Indian summer" ... in November. Changing closets invariably means sorting through clothes: studying some items before the full-length mirror for colors, hems, styles, general repair, etc. A mirror is a very handy fashion gauge - perhaps more so than the fashion magazines. My eyesight may be declining, so the reflection is usually useful: some fashion holdovers don't work!

Ephesians 5 is also quite a handy gauge for the Christian who is excited about his or her new identity and wants to please God. I need to banish some vestiges of the former me. For example, in my spiritual wardrobe, immorality of any kind, impurity of any kind, and greed are out. Obscenity, foolish talk, and coarse joking look especially bad on the Christian, no matter what the "season" is. Praise and thanksgiving are flattering outfits; even more attractive is understanding the Lord's will and laying aside foolishness.

No, we don't have to compare our wardrobes with any other Christian. The Lord knows what each of His children should be wearing and when. Christ is my pattern, and He's the person I pray we reflect. If we are good imitators, just maybe some people we love will ask the Lord to help them sort out their closets!

Still on the Battlefield

Israel faced an enemy who disabled the army and crippled the nation with fear (I Samuel 17). Goliath was an insulting and unrelenting threat to the nation's well-being. No one, from the King on down, believed they could defeat him, and no one remembered the Lord's unfailing promises to His people. Fearing man, the Israelites lost sight of their God. Fear of failure can disable me to the point where I cower, blinded and forgetful, as surely as the Israelites did.

In all of Israel, only one person, a youth, recognized the nature of the battle. David knew His God, and he remembered that the circumstances of his life were occasions in which the Lord had acted to deliver him. He trusted God to deliver him again, and an uncircumcised Philistine's defiance of the armies of the living God did not terrify him.

However, David also knew another man's armor, even the King's, would not protect him when he faced the enemy. He must use what he had and arm himself with what the Lord had trained him to use -- a sling. He went against a brute, perhaps four or five times his size, in the name of the Lord Almighty, the God of the armies of Israel, whom Goliath defied. David knew the battle was the Lord's.

What are you facing? Does it feel like a battle to you? Real and unrelenting? How does YOUR armor fit? Are you wearing what God commands, or did you borrow your gear from someone you admire? If you haven't chosen to dress yourself prayerfully and deliberately as the Lord commands in Ephesians 6:13-17, you might find yourself cornered, floundering around in someone else's armor and that will not suffice for your battle.

If we are battling with our kids, what is the issue, and what is the Lord's opinion and solution? Ask His advice. The Lord is very much interested in our children's character. He is also interested in how we go about building an environment to nurture them. Or have you only sought the opinion of "experts?" While there may be value in the advice of many counselors, seek the Lord's opinion first!

Read Psalm 131, and consider again what you are doing and why.

Did You *Ask* for a Kingdom?

Receiving a gift gracefully is an art, especially when the gift isn't quite what we would have chosen for ourselves. Underneath our Christmas tree is always a present that is not at the top of my Christmas "wish" list. Though unseen, it is very real. It is a kingdom, a precious gift from my God to me, because He loves me in the Beloved:

"Therefore since we receive a kingdom that cannot be shaken, let us show gratitude, by which we may offer to God an acceptable service with reverence and awe; for our God is a consuming fire." Hebrews 12:28-29.

I am sad to say that my flesh does not gracefully receive even the gift of a kingdom, knowing that a consuming fire accompanies the gift. The comfortable things of my life, however "good," might get burned up! This isn't always what I *want*.

Often what I want from God isn't "bad." I want a few extra hours to finish all the work for the Lord that I plan to do. I want extra money so I can give generously. I want children who will so live their lives that everyone will marvel at the wonders of Christian home school. I want a husband who is not so bushed, so we can wholeheartedly give ourselves to an important ministry that will truly help to preserve and advance the Christian faith in our country. Instead, the Lord gives a kingdom.

Because He loves me, He humbled himself, even to death on the cross, to be the sin offering for me so I could share with Him this wonderful kingdom. A friend

46

challenged me recently by asking, "How much do you want God to love you? Do you want Him to love you enough to change you?"

She then related a succinct story about her youngest son, that illustrates my "fleshly" response to God's gift. On a recent excursion in the car, he couldn't see the point of strapping on his seat belt for such quick jaunt. She stressed to him the purpose of the seat belt was to protect him by restraining him, and it came from her mother's heart of love. Glancing in the mirror, she saw her young son's disgruntled expression that seemed to say, "I wish you didn't love me that much!"

I am glad that God delivered me from the power of darkness and translated me into the kingdom of His dear Son (Colossians 1:13). Yet too often my flesh kicks against the goads (Acts 26:14). Like that small boy, I too, may be convinced that I am strapped too tightly for so short a journey! I am ashamed that, often, in the Lord's rear view mirror, I am annoyed at the restraints that come from the Father's heart of love.

God's gift of a kingdom isn't something to take out of a prettily wrapped box, admire, and lay aside, content to "own" a precious possession. Receiving his gift means sitting still long enough to open and appreciate it. It means laying aside the things that prevent me from receiving the new and better gift, and that keep me from firmly taking hold of the hand He extends.

He wants to walk with me through the Kingdom as my guide and comforter. And He wants me to open my hand and let go of what I am clutching so that He *can* hold my hand. Some days I might need to be "strapped in tightly," because I am so prone to wander from the God I love, even if I am doing the "work" of the kingdom. That consuming fire is as much for my good as the kingdom is a delight. I need that painful fire for it consumes the dross from my life:

"For those whom the Lord loves He disciplines, and He scourges every son whom He receives ... For what son is there whom his father does not discipline? . . . For [our earthly fathers] disciplined us for a short time as seemed best to them, but He disciplines us for our good, that we may share His holiness. All discipline for the moment seems not to be joyful, but sorrowful; yet to those who have been trained by it, afterwards yields the peaceful fruit of righteousness . " Hebrews 12:6-12

May we be grateful recipients of so great a salvation and rejoice one with another:

"For unto us a child is born, unto us a son is given: and the government shall be upon His shoulder. And his name shall be called Wonderful, Counselor, the Mighty God, the everlasting Father, the Prince of Peace. " (Handel's paraphrase of Isaiah 9:6)

Don't Forget the One Who Prays for You

"Ask and it shall be given to you; seek, and you shall find; knock, and it shall be opened to you. For everyone who asks receives, and he who seeks finds, and to him who knocks the door shall be opened. " Matthew 7:7-8

January and February loom ominously after the festive Christmas season. Facing a mountain of school work and chores, I worry if colds and flu will disrupt my schedule. I fret that inclement winter weather will be more than I can gracefully endure. Yet a blessed New Year is before me; one made hopeful by the scriptural invitation to ask, and the scriptural promise of answered prayer.

I'm not very spiritual if I begin to get frazzled - often the consequence of poor health and cabin fever. Instead of improving, my prayer life fades. My prayers become very self-absorbed, no longer seeking God's will. Full of self pity, I forget what I know about God, and become childishly convinced I *need* the things I want *now*! God says that He accepts me as his child through faith in Christ, but I wonder if He wants a more grown-up child.

Fortunately, my self absorption doesn't keep God from dealing with me. . . Fortunately, I have Jesus to pray on my behalf, and He prays very well (Hebrews 7:25). He is a friend to people like me who grapple with sin (Matthew 11:19). He is my friend because I

49

genuinely want to do what He commands (John 15:15). He wants to speak to me even when I'm not doing very well (Matthew 6:9). In my low spirits, He still whispers to me: "Pray and show me you trust me to respond."

When I accept the invitation to pray - to ask - I become aware of how generous and kind He is. "God, You provide my needs without my even knowing them. You give generously to one who can never repay. You answer my prayers even when they are shallow and selfish, and You let me that know you still value our relationship!"

If you, too, have failed to utter vibrant prayers because of viruses, days of cold, wet clothes, or unfinished lessons and chores, then think about the God to whom you are praying. He sees, hears, thinks, loves and cares. He knows what delights and pleases you . . . He is able to redeem the time that seems to slip away, to renew ebbing spirits, to heal tired bodies, and fill empty wallets. He can replenish a barn that the locusts have plundered. He will take time to comfort you, wipe away your tears, and rejoice with you. If you feel unworthy of His notice, remember He says you are more worthy than the sparrow whose fall to earth He also notices.

God has invited you and me to ask. Ask and give Him cause to provide the best answer. Ask now to receive not a wet, troubled, wheezy January and February, but a God-blessed commencement of the New Year!

How Do You Face an Invading Army With a $3 Defense Program?

What do you anticipate when you study God's word? This little poem is a stinging commentary that captures an unfortunate approach to Bible study and devotions that I recognize!

"$3.00 Worth of God"

By Wilbur Rees

"I would like to buy $3.00 worth of God, please - not enough to explode my soul or disturb my peace, but enough to equal a cup of warm milk or a snooze in the sunshine. I don't want enough of God to make me love an enemy; I want ecstasy, not transformation; I want the warmth of the womb; not a new birth. I want a pound of the Eternal in a paper sack. I would like to buy $3.00 worth of God, please."

If you have been hoping to manufacture just enough spirituality to get by, it is my prayer you will want to ask for a whole lot more of God - and that you will not be tempted to put Him in a paper sack!

Jehoshaphat, King in Judah almost 3,000 years ago, has shown me afresh the ways of our God . . . A friend brought his name up when she asked me to form a *praise choir* while she had to walk through some uncertain times with her precious child. I opened my hymnal and began to sing. Suddenly, I knew what the words "God inhabits the praise of His people" (Psalm 22:3) meant! Keeping my hymnal opened has changed my Bible study dramatically.

Please read for yourself 2 Chronicles 20. Jehoshaphat faced disaster after years of doing the right thing before the Lord. Facing powerful enemies, Jehoshaphat took his eyes *off* his circumstances, and looked to God. Consequently he led all Judah to see the deliverance that the Lord worked. Three dollars worth of the Eternal could not have defended Judah, nor is a paper sack full of God enough for us.

We can expect opposition when we try to trust and obey God. Don't yield and throw in the towel. Consider Jehoshaphat, and *stop* doing whatever consumes your day. Like Jehoshaphat, lay it out before the Lord and acknowledge you are powerless against the advancing army. Like Jehoshaphat, we have an audience. Our children, our family, or our neighbors are watching. Start to sing His praises, and you will taste victory over whatever might be separating you from Him!

As the Lord answered and assured them, so He answers and assures us - *the battle belongs to the Lord!* Twice He told them, "Do not fear, or be dismayed . . . for the battle is not yours, but God's." 2 Chronicles 20:15 How often are we disabled by fear and discouragement? These twin terrors are big distractions to completing our tasks, aren't they?

Has rumor of an invasion reached you? Your God *will* fight for you. Remember, if you have humbled yourself before Him claiming His Lordship, then whatever touches you touches God. Now, take up your position and take your eyes off your circumstances.

Have faith in the Lord your God and you will be upheld. Have faith in His prophets, and you will succeed. Stand firm and see what the Lord will enable you to do.

It is *immeasurably more* than you could think to ask of Him! (Ephesians 3:20) Oh yes, open your hymnal when you open your Bible and become a praise choir to splendor of God's holiness. Praise the One who will set ambushes for your enemies, and will give "plunder."

God inhabits the praise of His people, not a paper sack!

The Crown's Jewel

"If we judge by the world's standards, we will suffer the world's griefs and disappointments. " Author unknown.

Catering to a woman's sense of well-being is a major industry. Possessions and professions, husbands and children, exercise and diets are hawked as cures for what ails us. Even advertisements for some homeschool programs leave the distinct impression that peace, order, and prosperity are possible with the purchase from a certain company. When was the last time however we were urged just to be content in our circumstances? Young or old; single or married; healthy or ill; poor or rich, *be satisfied!* Contentment, even for women in the church, isn't usually our ambition, no matter how desperately we need it!

Clear away the stacks of books, fold the laundry, and wash up the last pot soaking in the sink, and what do we see? Do we see disgruntled children, with frowning faces? Do we find Mom busy reading about *how to find fulfillment*, or chatting with friends about her circumstances? Is the children's discontentment related to Mom's restlessness and dissatisfaction? Our goal as Christian wives and mothers is not simply an outward cheerful deportment, but a heart that is happy because it is surrendered and contented heart. Such a heart is *not* second nature, is it?

Recently I heard a speaker who addressed this poorly understood and seemingly elusive virtue: "Contentment - Christian Contentment." Nancy Wilson, a pastor's wife, mother and writer for the magazine *Credenda/Agenda*, asked us to consider "What is the view of my home, from my home?"

Nancy based her remarks on the seventeenth century classic, *The Rare Jewel of Christian Contentment* by a decidedly un-90's author, Jeremiah Burroughs. Learning contentment must be the continuing theme of our lives if we are to escape becoming women with "thread-bare souls, beneath a silken appearance." Employing Mr. Burroughs' characterization of contentment, Nancy began: *"Christian contentment is that sweet, inward, quiet, gracious frame of spirit, which freely submits to and delights in God's wise and fatherly disposal in every condition."*

Nancy then described some ways we women resist submitting to God's will. We often struggle to accept what comes from our Lord's hand, and are unwary of ingratitude, (Ephesians 5:20). We grumble, and *grumbling* is a prideful arrogance that assumes we somehow deserve better than what our Lord has provided. We sometimes do the very thing we don't like our children to do. We whine -- or murmur. Murmuring distracts from the duties God has ordained for us.

Sometimes our careless words may cause others to murmur. Have you ever heard the following careless words?

- "Are you pregnant *again* dear?" These words are not always supportive to one coping with an unexpected blessing.
- "Can't you *afford* ... ?" This question doesn't strengthen a woman's willingness to live within the budget of her husband's income, does it?
- "Why can't you understand this math [or grammar]? *Your sister [brother] has no trouble understanding it!*" Such caustic comparisons don't

motivate properly, and may stoke the fires of sibling rivalry that explode into bickering and arguments!

Christian contentment does not preclude beseeching the Lord for one's heart's desire. However, a contented heart is one that daily aligns its aspirations with its circumstances. Therefore, while we may ache for things, we would do well to crave more the fullness of His presence throughout the day. Mr. Burroughs declares, "when the heart is full of God, a little world goes a long way."

Nancy then offered an example of an impoverished woman, who while giving thanks for her scrap of bread, cried *"All this and Christ, too!"* This is a temperate but timely rebuke to one whose possessions do not bring contentment. Truly, thankfulness for what we have keeps us from being greedy for what the Lord may not want us to have (Hebrews 13:5).

As she finished her remarks, Nancy encouraged us to avoid comparisons to other women, because God doesn't intend to leave any of us the way we are. Instead, we should cultivate a teachable heart. Rejoice in one woman's strengths, and try to learn from her. Grieve for another's failures, and try to learn also.

When events threaten to overtake us, Nancy suggested making two lists. First, list the hardships, and be specific. Second, list the mercies God has shown. Again, be specific, because counting mercies transforms that little list of "wrongs" into a personal hymn of praise. Our trials and afflictions come to conform us to Christ's image: "They are a mercy to us." Finally Nancy quoted from one saint who exhorts believers, in "the cellar of affliction, to look for the choice wine!"

When Does Your "School" End?

I've collected some nifty gardening books chock
full of diagrams, pictures and charts - everything the
earnest gardener needs for success. Unfortunately my
zeal to dig, weed and plant is greater than my ambition
to study what the experts suggest. Somehow I never
seem to have enough time to master the material. Not
surprisingly, though I am enthusiastic, I can't produce
spectacular gardens. Unfortunately, undisciplined
enthusiasm blooms in other aspects of my life.

Zeal unrestrained by diligent study can overpower
my Christian walk. In the years I've been a Christian, I
have collected Bibles and several study aids. However,
these benefit me little until I actually study them. Until I
take the time to apply them to my situation, I have not
mastered anything except how to decorate a bookshelf.

Similar to the collection of Bibles and study
material is my accumulation of homeschooling aids.
Every year I am fascinated with the diversity and
usefulness of materials that are currently available.
Owning creative, engaging curricula, however, does not
assure thoroughly educated students *if* I skip over the
time to prepare and adapt material to our unique
requirements. Collecting imaginative teaching aids and
abandoning them on the shelf beside the gardening books
and Bibles will yield no more of a harvest in our school
than in backyard!

A study program that tickles my fancy or piques
my curiosity may not offer the lessons the Lord intends
for any of us in our family. Have I spent as much time

finding out His agenda as I have spent reviewing math texts? Collecting effective curriculum plans begins and ends with prayer, making time to seek the Lord's counsel.

Selecting clever material does not guarantee children will readily assimilate it. Nor does emphasizing my favorite subjects and ignoring the difficult ones produce thriving students. Home education that is unsystematic or lopsided can stunt the growth of students as certainly as too much sun and too little water in the garden.

Rushing and neglecting meditation and prayer endanger my "spiritual garden," and therefore threaten our educational garden - defeating the purpose of homeschooling. Also remember, all those beautiful books, easy-to follow plans, and foolproof projects will yield disappointing results if the teacher is unprepared or lacks direction from the Lord.

There *is* time to pray and prepare. The conveniences and appliances of twentieth century life make many more hours available for time with God and Scripture than my Mom had. In fact, I have the same number of hours to study as the Bereans, (Acts 17:11), and far fewer chores! A successful fall term will grow out of time spent in prayer, study and preparation, just as surely as a fruitful garden grows out of carefully prepared and tended soil.

"Summer School"

This summer some friends and I are studying the book of Isaiah. It has become clear why Isaiah is the most frequently quoted of the Old Testament prophets by the New Testament writers. He illustrated the Holy One of Israel in understandable images of Jesus Christ. Isaiah *saw* the Holy One of Israel, and then revealed in visionary flashes the mercy and majesty, the righteousness and wrath of the Lord.

More than this, Isaiah grabs my attention with little zingers, comments that literally take my breath because he has so accurately described something in *my* life! For example, when I sense my world shaking and collapsing around me, Isaiah gives his people AND me a precious nugget of truth about God.

"And He shall be the stability of your times, a wealth of salvation, wisdom, and knowledge; the fear of the Lord is His treasure." Isaiah 33:6

What does the promise of Isaiah 33:6 offer an exhausted, worn out homeschooling mom? Rest, glorious rest. Rest in the comfortable knowledge that Isaiah saw that the Holy One of Israel never slumbers, so that we might. He is *always* working to devise ways that He may bless, protect, purify, train, equip, restore, renew - and return us to the exact place where He wants us to serve!

Isaiah didn't limit the promise of security to only those unfavorable circumstances when nothing seems right. The Holy One of Israel will be the stability of my times - *whatever they are* - unfavorable, or favorable! The world sees health, education, money, companionship, position or privilege as essential for "stability." Isaiah sees it differently. The Holy One of Israel, He, will be the stability of my times - not more money, not obedient, super-spiritual, brilliant children, not health and happiness or a fancy degree!

May I encourage you who are exhausted? Using Isaiah's thoughts, may I strengthen you who are "feeble" after pouring your heart into another year of homeschooling? (Doesn't that perfectly describe your energy level after the last text was closed?) May I calm you who are anxious about the direction your life may be heading this summer?

> *"Take courage, fear not. Behold your God will come with vengeance,* [to protect and preserve you]; *the recompense of God will come,* [He will repay your labor in the Lord for your children's sake.] ... *But He will save you."* Isaiah 35:3-5

Until the Lord comes again His mouth has commanded, and His word has promised gladness, rejoicing, flourishing. Even if we think we are in the desert again, (not the easiest place to live, right?), we can bloom with assurance. *Rest*, lean way back on those everlasting arms. They will not fail you!

New Clothes

"Praise is becoming to the upright." Psalm 33:1

Christ's ambassadors need to be spiritually "well-dressed." So homeschooling moms, even if serving around the dining room table or kitchen, should be "attractive" to others for the sake of Christ. If spring is a perfect time to spruce up our wardrobes, putting aside what doesn't fit or flatter and adding something new, it is also a good time to check through our spiritual wardrobe. During these lengthening sunny days, will you eliminate some attitudes and habits that are not becoming, or appropriate on believers in the Lord Jesus Christ?

Sorting Out Your Outfits
Psalm 33:1 declares a pattern of spiritual grooming that is always becoming on the believer - inside or outside the home. Put on what truly becomes; *praise.*
"Sing for joy in the Lord, O you righteous ones; Praise is becoming to the upright. Give thanks to the Lord with the lyre; Sing praises to Him with a harp of ten strings. Sing to him a new song; Play skillfully with a shout of joy. For the word of the Lord is upright; and all his work is done in faithfulness. " Psalm 33:1-5
Our praise tells people what we believe about the Lord: His worth, His glory, His praise-worthy deeds. Do you believe all His work is done in faithfulness? Do you believe He is faithfully at work today in your circumstances?

61

What I believe about God shows as clearly as drooping hems, ripped seams, spotted clothes and untidy hair.

What has the Lord wrought in your life recently? Are you unable to praise God wholeheartedly in your present circumstances? Do you have more responsibilities and chores than time to do them? Are your bills bigger than your budget? Is your child ill? Have your schooling plans crashed to defeat because one of your children refuses to obey, two don't care, and one simply doesn't grasp the work? Is your husband hardly ever at home because of his job? Has your teen-ager gotten his license, and now *drives*? Praise is not always our first reaction, nor is praise always easy. However our response to our experiences expresses what we believe, and what we believe about God shows in our demeanor.

Choose the New Stuff!

"Dressing well" spiritually means we first take off old familiar costumes, and put on Christ's righteous robes -- *daily*. It means we willingly confess there is nothing in our wardrobe to cover our soul's nakedness. He must remove our shame and cover us with His glory. Next we put on what is truly becoming: *praise*.

Just as dressing well requires thought and time, so developing spiritual habits of praise requires thought and time. The praise that is embodied in Psalms requires contemplation and communion with God. If putting on make-up and adjusting hems is risky when we rush, so is spiritual grooming. Praise is not a quick glance in the mirror and a hollered out, "thanks, Lord" as I rush about my chores, or fly out the door to my next good deed.

62

"New Clothes" Aren't Always Comfortable!

We may be uncomfortable at first in our spiritual "new clothes," especially in trying or tedious circumstances, and we may catch ourselves slipping into something more comfortable. Interruptions, obstacles, setbacks, and defeats can chafe our spirits and we long for relief. Grumbling, yelling, sulking, slamming doors, or cursing may feel "comfortable," like slipping into sweat pants and sneakers from a suit and heels. But who enjoys being caught slouching about in old clothes? If old clothes convey an image we shun, how much more should we rue getting caught in sloppy vestiges of the old self! "Old" spiritual outfits may feel comfortable because they are familiar, but beware! When we are found in them they reveal the remains of the spiritual "hags" Christian women once were.

Rage, malice, slander and filthy language suit the "old" woman; the woman, *before* Christ, who was as ugly and abrasive as the "hags" who horrified Shakespeare's MacBeth. They do not fit the new creation I have become. (2 Corinthians 5:17)

Though she is conquered, the hag of my old nature can still meddle, murmuring to distract me from habits of praise and worship. Soon, I may stop looking in the mirror of Scripture and begin listening to one who would keep me in unflattering sloppy outfits. The *old* woman encourages me to relax and slip into my "old clothes" -- an attitude that is comfortable, but corrupt; a habit that is familiar, but depraved. Have you ever heard her?

"How can you be thankful for *that*? Put away those new clothes, dear," she hisses. "Save them for church or a party. You don't want to soil them, working so hard for all these ungrateful people!"

Our new outfits may pinch and bind, because we are trying to stuff a few pounds of that *old woman* into the new garments. Yet they will come to fit us perfectly, if we *keep growing* in Christ and the knowledge of the Word. We may fret and wonder if Christ's robes are our "color," but if we persist He will prove His choice is *very becoming*.

"New Clothes" Are A Choice

Whether in quietness or chaos, we can deliberately choose how to dress because we know we are continually in the presence of the Lord of creation. We can be temperate and restrained in our speech and actions because we know we are in the company of the people He has determined to be our circle of acquaintances. We can be resolute to praise and worship the Lord, even when the old woman badgers us to stay in the old clothes and skip devotions or sleep late Sunday, because we know the Lord means for our demeanor to be *attractive*.

Still can't find *a thing* to wear? Try these on for size. The Psalmist encourages believers to be elaborate with their praise ... to make music ... to make our praise new. As the Lord's faithfulness is new every morning, so our praise should be alive, fresh and vibrant. Sing, praise, give thanks, play skillfully, with a shout of joy! Such praise looks *good* on believers.

Sing -- yes aloud -- love songs to God, delighting to name His attributes, *believing* that He listens. Use the Psalms, a hymnal or praise tapes. Think about what your "brothers" and "sisters" sang to the Lord.

Remember what is in your life because of the Lord's faithfulness. Be mindful of what your faithful God has kept out of your life!

Bless God for His wisdom in giving to you your husband and your children. Praise God, in your husband's presence, for him and what he means to you. Praise God, in your children's presence, for each by name.

Be grateful that you *have* a chore list, even if it seems beyond your powers to complete. Chores mean the Lord trusts you. He has entrusted work into your hands, even if the work is diapers, dishes and dusting. Doing simple work well can lead to great things. *"And whatever you do, whether in word or deed, do it in the name of the Lord Jesus, giving thanks to God the Father through him."* Colossians 3:17

How can He trust you with Kingdom work, if you grumble about daily work?

Thank God for your budget constraints. Through them He can teach you dependence upon Himself alone, and stewardship. What more effective way to learn of His unfailing kindness, than to be taught through His satisfaction of genuine need?

Your New Ensemble Is a Free Gift

As we count the cost of faithfulness, remember that Someone else paid for our robes. Especially at Easter let praise, the perfect adornment, pour forth and complete our new outfits. Loving and lavish praise seems the only sensible response to the gift of salvation. Praise of the Lord Jesus Christ both acknowledges the Designer of our new ensemble, and directs those who are watching us to consider His patterns for themselves. When we are praising Jesus Christ, everyone -- even our kids and husbands -- will see that we are incredibly better dressed than when we wore our *former* at-home apparel.

A Pithy Proverb: Better Than a Daily Planner!"

"So, teach us to number our days, that we may present to Thee a heart of wisdom. " Psalm 90:12

This beloved phrase is often quoted, especially to folks caught up in the "tyranny of the urgent." What do we mean when we ask God to teach harried women or beleaguered men to number their days? How does "numbering our days" build a heart of wisdom, anyway?

To begin, merely subtracting our birth year from the present year is a heart-stopping education. If our life span is 70 or 80 years, then "middle-age" is really about 35 or 40. How's *that* for a wake-up call? Still, journeying across four or five decades, we do pick up knowledge; some we can confidently share.

For example, parents whose children are leaving home can quite honestly tell anxious new parents to relax. Enjoy the days of grubby little hand prints, scraped knees and toothless grins, for they are soon ended. Men and women on the downward slope of 40 can counsel busy couples to consider how they are allocating their time between family and job. Veteran homeschoolers will confirm that *years* of unnecessary disquiet over academic lessons were costly. Worrying, they frittered away precious hours of fellowship with the Lord and time to disciple their children.

Some of us have sadly discovered, gaining a heart of wisdom often comes *after* there are very few days left to number! So, the psalmist seems to mean more than heeding how swiftly time passes. The psalmist reminds us that numbering our days aright produces a wise heart. A wise heart is a heart that is useful to God.

Source Of An Old Saw

Moses wrote this psalm. Even as a young man, and a well-educated prince in Pharoah's court, Moses had a short fuse. In anger, he murdered an Egyptian who was abusing a Hebrew slave. Subsequently Moses spent forty years continuing his education in radically different circumstances, until God gave him an unusual commission. The Lord asked Moses to liberate a multitude of Hebrew slaves and lead them into the "Promised Land." The ungrateful Hebrew slave, whose life Moses had defended years earlier, was an apt personification of the group God had in mind to be led to freedom.

Vacillating, ungrateful and willful, the Hebrews tested Moses intellectually and exasperated him spiritually. Matthew Henry, the seventeenth century English commentator, writes that Moses may have penned the words of Psalm 90:12 when the Lord passed sentence on Israel for their *unbelief, murmuring* and *rebellion* in the wilderness. (Numbers 14) Moses knew what it was to number days, having spent 40 years tending sheep.

Therefore, recollecting the Lord's severe mercy, Moses now asked the Lord, "teach us to number our days, that we may present to Thee a heart of wisdom." Moses believed human hearts could change, if the Lord would teach them how to count.

Like Fathers, Like Sons ... and Daughters

Why were the Israelites grumbling? Though dramatically spared from death, freed from Egyptian oppression and led out of bondage with much wealth, they still cowered when they realized they faced a struggle to secure what the Lord promised them. Preoccupied with fear, they doubted God's faithfulness in the face of trouble (Numbers 13:30-33).

Like Israel, we can risk abandoning ourselves to unbelief when God delays answering our petitions. Modern Americans tend to feel it permissible to vent frustrations - "to share what is troubling us" - and this tendency has seeped into the Church. Verbalizing our troubles may quickly wax into grumbling and murmuring, the same sins for which God punished Israel. Grumbling represents doubt and rebellion against the Lord.

The Israelites' griping eventually infuriated Moses past the point of patience (Numbers 20:11), causing him to strike rather than speak to the rock as God had commanded. By doing that, he forfeited leading the assembly into the land God gave them. Moses, therefore, would understand our frustrations in leading smaller flocks of the Lord's lambs.

Rebels Can Provoke Downfall of More than Governments

Rebellious people provoke real trouble. Our children can be exasperating, for until Christ frees them they are the bondservants of Satan. Even afterward, they tend (like us) to argue and resist authority. Resistance takes many forms, but rebellion eventually pushes parents to the point of exasperation.

Exasperation cost Moses the privilege of possessing the fruit of his labors. Similarly, exasperated homeschooling parents may squander their authority and opportunities to train their children spiritually. A sputtering, red-faced, hysterical mom is not a credible witness for the power of the indwelling Holy Spirit, is she? A fuming, furious dad cannot teach his children effectively from the word of God, can he?

Applying an Antique Adage

If looking at Moses' leadership can strengthen leadership in our home, what can we learn from the Israelites' resistance? The "Nephilim" that terrified Moses' spies have counterparts in unpleasant surprises we encounter in the "Promised Land" of homeschooling. Is there a similarity in our response?

The Israelites wailed at the reports of Moses' spies returning from Canaan. Though Caleb argued they could go up and take possession, the people -- forgetting their astonishing deliverance from Egypt -- cried, wept and grumbled against Moses, proclaiming their wish to have died in Egypt or in the wilderness! They accused God of bringing them into this place so they might fall by the sword, and complained that their wives and children would be taken as plunder. They even regarded going back under the yoke of slavery a sensible plan when compared with advancing into the land the Lord promised as their inheritance.

New homeschoolers, who enthusiastically embrace the dreams of homeschooling, may be astounded to discover the extent of their new daily tasks. Suddenly they realize their youngsters, who can sing each of the TV character Barney's songs, can't remember how to spell "cat" or retain the most elementary math facts. They are bewildered when their children don't care for

69

the academic freedom they now have, and only hanker for their former school chums. The kids often are not grateful to pursue a custom-made academic program and may resist doing *any* school work! Slowly it begins to dawn on homeschooling parents that the Lord, by calling them to homeschooling, expects them to educate these children despite their attitudes!

Are veteran homeschooling moms *less* likely to murmur? Perhaps a bit, but we also have been known to weep and wail and moan loudly, haven't we? Forgetting how faithfully the Lord has rescued, protected and directed us in the past, we often falter when facing new struggles. We ignore encouragement to go and take possession, and we, too, cower fearing failure.

Avoiding the Desert's Traps

Should we expect the Lord miraculously to transport us to high school graduation, like our ancestors expected Him to convey them into the Promised Land painlessly? Of course not! Why then are we quick to charge Him with leaving us in disarray, amid rowdy children who are insolent and apathetic? Why do we refuse to advance by faith, trusting the Lord who has led thus far? Why, in exasperation with the demanding duty of building character (theirs and ours), do we toy with the idea of returning the children to the same kind of school from which God deliberately led our families out?

Loving, teaching, disciplining, forgiving, and encouraging our children are what God does, and that is what He wants us to do. Matthew Henry comments that Moses was asking God to teach His people how few our days on earth are, "... and how little a while we have to live in this world. We must so number our days as to compare our work with them, and mind it accordingly

with double diligence, as those that have no time to
trifle. Those that would learn this arithmetic must pray
for divine instruction."

Consider A *Re*-Commissioning

Do you believe each day is a day of divine instruction for
you and your children? Years ago, a young mother's
violent and sudden death showed me that numbering my
days is more than "marking time." One dreary winter's
day, she relinquished her career as a wife and mother
unexpectedly, because the brakes of an eighteen-wheeler
failed right behind her car at the intersection of two busy
thoroughfares. She went home to glory, leaving her
achievements ambitions, and the nurturing of her beloved
children to others.

By God's grace, most of us will not leave life so
young or so suddenly, but her tragic death can remind us
how little time we have to labor for the Lord, to enjoy
our children, family and friends, and even to grapple
with the "giants." Each day is a fresh opportunity to
number our days diligently, measuring our daily work by
how well we used the hours God gave us, remembering
we have no throw-away time to murmur, grumble or
trifle. Each day, whatever the limits, is a day of divine
instruction, to build in us a heart of wisdom.

Are You Willing To Be Taught?

"The Teacher is here," she said, "and He is calling for you." John 11:28

Though she wistfully acknowledged His power to change the situation when she went out to meet Jesus, Martha, Lazarus' sister, nevertheless charged Him with her brother's death. Her indictment of the Lord because of His "absence" is not so different from ours, is it? How often have we greeted the Lord with "if you had been here Lord, none of this would have happened?" We complain that God was away, and therefore our world collapsed around us. If He really was watching, this present calamity would never have befallen us. John's detailed account of events before the Lord's mighty raising of Lazarus from the dead shows however that "Christ never brings his people into any peril but He accompanies them in it ... Christ is a faithful guide in all our doubts, and a powerful guard in all our dangers."

Possibly Martha was tired. She had buried her brother, having attended him as he lay dying. While many Jews had come to mourn the death of Lazarus and support the family, they probably added to Martha's responsibilities. Maybe Martha was disappointed. She had asked for help from the only One she trusted could help, but He tarried, deliberately staying away from the one He loved, her brother Lazarus.

Her sister Mary sat in the house. What was on her mind? Was she pouting because Christ did not answer her request for Him to come, even after she had sat diligently at His feet to learn? Did the friends of her family discourage her from going to Christ? Did she prefer to nurture her grief instead of cultivating her faith?

Though they were close companions of the Lord Jesus, Martha and Mary forgot who He was as easily as you and I can in grief and disappointment. "In the depths of affliction, let this therefore keep us out of the depths of despair, that man's extremity is God's opportunity."

Still, when Martha heard Jesus was coming, she went immediately to meet Him. Martha stepped outside the misery that had descended upon her life; she lay down the obligations that were multiplying and went to meet Jesus.

Jesus did not rebuke her when she assailed Him; He comforted her: "Your brother will rise again." Jesus thus began patiently and powerfully to teach her and the disciples who accompanied Him, about the hope of the resurrection they professed:

"I am the resurrection and the life; he who believes in Me shall live even if he dies, and everyone who lives and believes in Me shall never die. Do you believe this?" John 11:25-26

Martha believed this promise, and confessed Jesus to be the Christ, the Son of the Living God. Her first act after this astounding confession ... for a Jewish woman ... was to go privately to her sister, bound in grief and despair and tell her, "The Teacher is here, and He is calling for you." John 11:28

Maybe, like Martha and Mary, you have sustained a loss or a blow you believe the Lord could have deflected. Or, maybe you want to comfort loved ones in

73

distressing circumstances. No one escapes being splashed with the debris of brokenness that saturates American life today. People's problems today appear overwhelming.

Where do we find answers for people caught in abusive marriages, or tangled in the chains of substance abuse? Does Scripture give hope today to folks coping with physical and mental disabilities? How can we encourage men and women struggling with the trauma caused by alcoholic or abusive parents? How can we encourage parents whose children have strayed from Christ to embrace the world? What can a Christian say to one who has lost his or her job and faces the consequences of consumer debt?

Martha can teach twentieth century believers how to make a difference to hurting people. First Martha was reconciled to Christ, then she began to comfort her sister by directing Mary to Christ. I have no reliable words of comfort if the solace of Christ has not quieted my soul. Matthew Henry says that the words "The teacher is here" are the "best cordial" in distress."

Moreover, he continues, "When Christ, our master comes, He calls for us. He calls for thee in particular, for thee by name. If He calls thee, He will cure thee, He will comfort thee." If Christians believe Christ is in the very midst of our troubles; that He knows us by name, we must be wary of giving "comfort" that distracts others from seeking Christ.

Because we are prone to undervalue our future hope, we are readily discontent in our circumstances. Worldly remedies, however helpful, can disrupt the lesson Christ intends to teach us. The world's answers may appear true, but don't they divert people from Christ? For example, the "Twelve Steps" of many self-help programs may guide a person to sobriety, but unfortunately also may walk a troubled, sober soul to a

Christ-*less* eternity. The so-called "inner-child" has a selective memory, and is unconcerned with the soul's eternal destiny. The One who formed the human heart is the only one to cure it.

Therefore, it is our duty, says Matthew Henry, to help those who mourn, to reconcile themselves to the will of God. "The crosses and comforts of this present time would not make such an impression upon us as they do," he writes, "if we did but believe the things of eternity as we ought."

The Teacher is not ignoring you in your troubles; He is with you; He is calling for you. He is able to do exceeding, abundantly beyond all we ask or think, according to the power that works within those who believe Him (Ephesians 3:20-21). Have you asked Him? Are you willing to be taught? Do you trust Him to do things His way?

PART THREE

Character

Flaws

Homeschooling Uncovered

"But now you also, put them all aside: anger, wrath, malice, slander, and abusive speech from your mouth ... Fathers, do not exasperate your children, that they may not lose heart." Colossians 3: 8, 21

Cain's Kinfolk

Do you know about the "big bang?" Sometimes at
our house the original roots of our family tree become
explosively obvious. Unfinished lessons and chores,
frustration, and fatigue intersect, then *bang*! I behold the
angry evidence of my ancestor - Cain. A murderous
hothead like Cain in *my* family's tree, how can this be?
Well, we do spring from the same seed, and the vein of
selfishness and self-centeredness that motivated Cain has
persisted through many generations down to me.

I like to think I am better than Cain - more
developed, perhaps - am I so different? Recognizing my
"earthly" genealogy, it follows naturally that the
bombshell of anger may well explode with stunning force
when my plans are thwarted or when I must refuse my
children their preferences.

The seeds of "ancestral" anger can bloom
unexpectedly, especially when I am frustrated. Confusion
is often anger's traveling companion, and when that duo
invade they wreak havoc. Stunned, I find myself looking
into a yawning black pit of unrestrained fury and
wondering, how did *that* get into my home and *how* can I
get it out? However, being related to Cain, doesn't mean
I have to ape him. Through the blood of Christ, God has
freed me from the power of harmful habits. Jesus Christ
is now my closest kin, not Cain.

A Wise Man's Recommendation
Solomon, a wise king and no stranger to the struggles of
the heart, spoke often of anger. He suggests exercising

"discretion" to subdue anger. *"A man's discretion makes him slow to anger, and it is to his glory to overlook a transgression. "* Proverbs 19:11 Discretion is not just zipping the lips, and it is more than sensitively relaying prayer requests!

Noah Webster defines *discretion* so as to almost suggest a path for me to follow when anger and confusion threaten to overrun my home. First, he says, *discretion* names an act - separation. Leave the room quietly, instead of continuing the dispute. Withdraw respectfully, but promptly, from any conversation that is becoming a shouting match. If "time-out" works for willful toddlers, why not try one for yourself? A quiet time to reflect privately, regain composure, and confess and repent, can deflate fury fast!

Second, *discretion* describes a faculty, which is discernment. Stop, draw back from the fray, and listen and watch. Pause long enough to understand how this argument got started. Stop talking (or yelling) and ask the Lord for wisdom! (James 1:5).

Third, *discretion* is the power of a free decision. If "choice" is such a hot ticket, exercise it! I choose to bridle my tongue. I choose to harness my emotions. I choose to honor God by how I am disciplining my children, instead of venting my frustration because they refuse to mind!

Finally, *discretion* connotes *prudence*, cautious reserve, especially in speech. Pause and reflect, "Would Jesus enjoy hearing the words that are about to spill from my tongue? Would my words or actions give Him glory?"

Defusing a Bomb, According to the Definition

You may not realize the destructive power of anger and confusion, if you have never experienced adoption into

God's family through faith in the Lord Jesus Christ. Or as a Christian, the dubious duo of anger and confusion may continually rob you of your joy. Defusing "anger" bombs is risky business. Consider asking for help from the expert bomb disposer.

As a member of God's family through faith in Jesus Christ, I now have the power to back off when I experience anger; to *separate*, before confusion gets a foothold. A prompt "quiet time," separate from the battle field, can restore sanity. *"He who is slow to anger has great understanding, but he who is quick-tempered exalts folly"* Proverbs 14:29

Next, we can practice discernment. Slow down and *listen*. Whose voice do we hear, telling us to do what? Would Jesus *say* or *do* what we are about to say or do? Now then, think about the tone of your voice. If you expressed your "opinions" first to Jesus before telling your children or husband, what would you say and how would you say it? *"A gentle answer turns away wrath, but a harsh word stirs up anger"* Proverbs 15:1

Finally, pick your battles. Overlooking a transgression does not mean it has escaped God's notice. Evaluate where this displeasure ranks on an eternal scale. When you stand before the Lord, will He be pleased you took a battle position on this troubling issue? *"This you know, my beloved brethren. But let everyone be quick to hear, slow to speak and slow to anger, for the anger of man does not achieve the righteousness of God."*

Do I follow my own good advice? Well, let's just say, the city has not yet been captured, but I *want* that victory, and am grateful Christ means for me to have it! (Proverbs 16:32)

Where Is Your Faith?

Sometime this school year your homeschooling boat may begin to take on water, especially if an unexpected storm whips up. Will you be swamped? You might sympathize with the disciples who told Luke their encounter with rough seas. Someone who was on that boat with the snoozing Savior told the good doctor emphatically, *they were in danger!* (Luke 8:22-25).

Stormy weather during homeschooling can be as frequent and as real as storms on the Sea of Galilee ... and just as terrifying. *Or did you think that homeschooling your kids would be as relaxing as a Caribbean cruise?* Surely the shock of a hurricane of emotions and a deluge of angry words at the dining room/school table has sent more than one Mom crying to the Lord, "We are perishing!" Like the disciples we often fear that He is sleeping, unaware of the rising water.

Your homeschooling plan may blow away two hours after you open the books this year, or hold steady until shortly before Easter. A waterspout may hit, unpredicted, originating from unexpected sources such as financial needs, health failures, fatigue, rebellious hearts, contrary attitudes, or academic burn-out because you overestimated talent, time or resources.

Remember, if Christ has invited you into the boat, He sets the course and promises His constant presence. He also takes responsibility for reaching the destination.

Not one gentle breeze or roof-ripping wind blows that the Lord Jesus Christ does not know of it and command its track.

You may be steering through financial shoal waters; you may be navigating treacherous emotional storms; you may be becalmed and drifting through endless chores and dull drills. However, He *is* in your boat if you are homeschooling at His direction, and you *will* hear Him ask, *"Where is your faith?"*

Whatever your "navigational" charts show, please remember: *Who* organized your homeschool voyage? Who plotted the course and provisioned the boat? Whose hand is on the tiller? Whose power fills your sails? If you answer any name except *Jesus*, you *will* be blown off course and are in imminent danger of being swamped! Having any other captain means you can't hold your course when the winds begin to blow. Christians cannot waiver between two opinions. *Who is in charge of your ship?*

Quit scrambling to get your homeschool plans shipshape in your own strength. Check your course against the Bible and take your position sightings from His word. Steer your course according to *the* Captain's orders, and wait expectantly for His next command.

STUNG!

Parents are students too. I learn this all the time. With all the bustle of new homeschool plans, books and projects this fall, I nearly overlooked an important lesson the Lord was trying to impress upon me. Thankfully, He is a persistent and innovative educator, using the problems He has permitted to come into my life to guide and instruct me, so I can teach.

For example, as school began, the Lord used an insect's nasty sting on my leg as effectively as a schoolmaster might rap the knuckles of a daydreaming student. That mystery insect's sting left an ugly swollen sore - the Lord's way of showing me how I had allowed exasperation and irritation to leave an ugly impression on my lessons. He is patiently teaching me that "reacting" rather than thoughtfully "responding" to problems of daily living wrecks learning in some of life's most important subjects.

I Can Teach By *Breathing* Funny

As a parent I am always teaching, even if the circumstances are not to my liking and even if the lessons are not what I intend. My response to circumstances, especially the unpleasant or unexpected, becomes a powerful lesson. Therefore, I need to learn how poisonous exasperation and irritation can be in home education. My exasperation and irritation can suddenly "poison" the best training opportunities, causing an "allergic" reaction, infecting the teacher and the student as quickly as the poison from an insect's stinger inflamed my leg. It took me a while to respond to the Lord's gracious but firm rap!

84

Fall Trips Over Summer

We began the day very smoothly. Congratulating myself on how well our lessons had gone *inside* the house, I popped outside and saw our yard was not so well organized. The glow of my excitement over our orderly commencement quickly faded as I surveyed the summer's undone chores. I had agreed to deferrals of various chores for good reasons: the heat, the upcoming vacation, etc. But, when chores are postponed they accumulate, and beholding an accumulation of undone chores can overload my circuits. Then I blow a fuse, and impatiently *do* the very work I'm trying to train the kids to do - because it seems easier. But "easier" isn't a good teaching goal.

It suddenly became my priority to get those "backlogged" jobs done immediately. I started my engine - never pausing to consider how I might use an unpleasant situation to teach. Roaring off, I never thought to ask the kids, or my husband, to do what they had agreed to do -- to share the load of keeping our home in good order. Ignoring our unanimously agreed-upon "chores chart" that assigns jobs to family members, I buzzed from the front yard to the back, becoming as harried as Alice's White Rabbit in Wonderland. Working feverishly and thinking only that these chores had to be done *now*, my heart became a tempting a target for Satan's fiery dart, just as my leg was a tempting target for the sting of an unseen bug.

A Bug for the Bugged

In my frenzy to tidy up the bedraggled backyard, I was only vaguely aware that something was crawling up my leg. I brushed it away, but not before the insect stung. Ouch! My exasperation doubled, but the painful sting didn't stop me. I whirled on to the next task, rebuffing my daughter's suggestion to stop and tend the reddening sore. I ignored her good advice just as I ignored the carefully planned chores chart, *and* the biblical remedy for the sting of displeasure. (See how to address the "guilty," Matthew 18). The poison from both stingers - spiritual and physical - festered.

My frenetic efforts in the yard did not succeed. I couldn't finish weeks of other people's jobs in a few minutes, especially when the skin around the bite swelled and my leg began to itch and ache. By evening I was plenty uncomfortable, and at this point I understood the Lord's lesson. When I looked at the puffy red skin I began to assess the cost of my exasperation, rung up at the expense of real learning.

My irritation over the "undone" chores had so inflamed me that I missed the opportunity to teach a useful lesson -- that even deferred chores remain the individual's responsibility. Instead I taught my kids -- "Mom, the whirling dervish, will swoop in and do it herself. No need to bother now to try to finish what I left undone."

I still don't know what kind of insect stung me, but I thank my God who saw me fussing around our yard and used a tiny unseen insect stinger to remind me of the real enemy who is prowling about to prey on my impatience. Chastened, I admitted to God I was more concerned about the appearance of a disorderly yard than about the lesson I would teach by my reaction to disorder.

I could have used the same circumstances to direct my children to follow through on their agreements to do chores. The lesson was not wasted, however. I learned my Teacher will waste no experience to teach me to bridle my irritable temper - a lesson I hope I don't have to learn often!

Letting Go

". . . [T]hese have been written that you may believe that Jesus is the Christ, the Son of God; and that believing you may have Life in His name. " John 20:31

When He lived among us, the Lord mingled with many people who listened to His teaching, even pursued Him, but did not yield to Him. Most folks who heard Jesus preferred their own opinions and conventions of living, to the "narrow path" He offered.

Some yielded, though. The Gospels recount many who surrendered. Two people, a man and a woman from opposite ends of the social spectrum, impressed the apostle John deeply. Their lives continue to intrigue readers of the New Testament 2,000 years later. Did they learn something that we need to know? Could a rendezvous with Christ make a difference in our homeschooling?

John tells first of the Pharisee who came to Jesus at night. Nicodemus, the Temple ruler, was initially an uneasy seeker. Important in the world's eyes, he later yielded his status and became an advocate for Christ before the Sanhedrin (John 7:50) and a compassionate friend who generously brought the ointments needed to bury Christ (John 19:39). Next, John details how an unnamed Samaritan woman went alone to the town's well to draw water and met the Lord "by chance" (John 4:6). Her transformation was immediate and persuasive - from a harlot to a powerful evangelist (John 4:28-30).

What can homeschooling parents learn from these two contemporaries of Christ? First, hopefully, we fall somewhere between the extremes of the highly placed ruler and the coarse Samaritan harlot. If a ruler can become a servant and a trollop an evangelist, can't Christ make homeschooling parents effective educators?

Next, home educators can surely cling to courses and curricula, pride, predilections and prejudices as tightly as Nicodemus initially clung to his position and the woman initially clung to her sin. Can Jesus change us as suddenly, as gently? Can He use us as powerfully? Can He equip us to train our children?

He can, but how willing are we to be changed? We *can* become effective educators *if* we are willing to let go of our own wisdom, and pursue God's. When we launched our homeschooling programs, we began with some preconceived notions (possibly even a fear of failure!) plus an agenda of educational goals for our children that may have overshadowed our spiritual objectives. Possibly we didn't grasp what the Bible teaches parents must do to train their children, nor plan accordingly.

Our homeschooling ambitions may have blinded us as completely as Nicodemus' pride corrupted his spiritual sight. Worse, our fear of failure may have hobbled us as completely as the woman's immorality limited her. We may still be clutching the world's definition of an education so tightly, we can't embrace the Teacher, who has promised never to leave or forsake us.

John the Baptist gave an uncomplicated pattern for change, which the apostle John notes. Referring to Jesus, John the Baptist said simply "He must increase and I must decrease." John 3:30 His simple, true words explain why Christ is often rejected, why Christian aspirations -- including homeschooling -- often flounder.

Christ increasing, "me" decreasing, might be a frightening proposition! Yet yielding control of our education goals to Christ is to share the spoils of His victory; to enjoy the inheritance He secured. Could any of our academic "victories" equal His triumph over sin and death? Could any scholarly "inheritance" we accumulate for our kids compare to the riches He has for them? Could our ambitions for our children compare to the fruitful lives He has planned for them - as well as the training and education that He WILL provide, if we ask His will?

If we could meet with Christ as Nicodemus or the woman did, how would the conversation go? Just as He rebuked the woman, He might warn us that we frequently go to the wrong "well" to satisfy our academic "thirst." He might wonder about our curriculum. Why do we spend so much time deciding which math book or grammar program suits our children, and so little time teaching character from the Bible? While we busily equip our children for, at best, a half-century of employment, do we intend to send them into eternity ignorant of their savior, He might ask.

If we will seek Christ, we will find He is waiting patiently; as patiently as He waited for Nicodemus and the woman at the well. The apostle John has written of their experiences with Christ so that we may know that the Lord deals effectively with all kinds of people. Surely He can teach us to teach. We can begin our lessons by simply *letting go*.

"June Cleaver" Didn't Throw the Silverware"

"Love ... does not act unbecomingly ... "
1 Corinthians 13:4-7

Thanks to television syndication, June Cleaver (of "Leave it to Beaver") is entertaining yet another generation of viewers. Like several TV Moms of the 1960s', June now suffers derision because we in the 1990s' dismiss her constant calm and unfailing charm as incredible. We ridicule her household management skills as impractical. However, the impression of her composure while she cared for her family still appeals to me, although I've never tried to scrub the kitchen floor wearing heels, pearls and a pencil slim skirt.

Granted, we children of the sixties only saw those TV moms briefly. Nevertheless, Barbara Billingsly, Harriet Nelson and Donna Reed were characters whose impressions have not faded from our contemporary consciousness - good, bad, or indifferent. Do you wonder about the impression you will leave upon your family? Twenty-five years from now, will the memory of your character be an indelible impression on your children?

Unlike fictional TV parents, Christian homeschooling parents can propagate spiritual fruit. But we must be wary. Like the Corinthians, even if we are the most gifted and skilled teachers, we risk being resounding gongs. Even if we possess the most erudite and creative curricula, and spend generous amounts of time with our children, *if we do not have love, we are nothing* -- without love, we profit nothing from the riches God bestows on us (See 1 Corinthians 13:1-3).

How God Got My Attention
Recently during morning devotions, we read the "Love" passage, 1 Corinthians 13. Gongs began clanging loudly in my ears as I recalled that only the evening before I had thrown down a handful of silverware, hotly riled because of a family "discussion." This morning I could hardly hear my husband's words as he read. *Love* had not been the unforgettable impression of that evening!

Traditionally Paul's message to the Corinthian church is recited during weddings. However, Paul was not discussing marriages, but was commending Jesus Christ to a young church whose members were behaving *unbecomingly*. Paul was reminding them of a still more excellent way to build their church, and his words apply equally to homeschoolers who may be looking everywhere but the Lord to build their homes.

Tired of the "Gong Show?"
Harmonizing homeschooling and homemaking can deplete our affection for our spouses and children. If we are not trusting the Father's love, we quickly exhaust our storehouse of natural affection. No matter our talents, if we insist on running on "empty" fuel tanks a cacophonous explosion is predictable, and our homes fill with noise and confusion like the defunct TV "Gong Show."

The solution Paul offered the Corinthians also quiets noisy twentieth century gongs. He tells the Corinthians, and us, we have the ideal of love to follow - Jesus Christ - and we have His power so we might conform to His example. *Love* is a gift from God to me for my children and husband. It is the glue that holds even the most precarious homeschooling programs together, and the oil that lubricates even the most-worn gears of debilitated home educators.

I looked again at Paul's temperate reproof to the Corinthians. Knowing I falter frequently, failing to display love's virtues, how can I apply the following verse?

"Love is patient, love is kind, and is not jealous; love does not brag and is not arrogant, does not act unbecomingly; it does not seek its own, is not provoked, does not take into account a wrong suffered, does not rejoice in unrighteousness, but rejoices with the truth; bears all thing, believes all things, hopes all things, endures all things. " 1 Corinthians 13:4-7

Perhaps you will see a pattern of Jesus Christ if you study this passage. Perhaps you will see the power God places at our disposal to quell the gongs.

Love is Patient ...
When I see what needs doing, and nothing is happening; *patience* isn't how I describe my frame of mind. Nevertheless, "Love can endure provocation, even evil, *without* being filled with resentment and rage," Matthew Henry comments. Love is serene and tolerant, forbearing disappointment and grief, because love knows first, that God is in control -- of spilt milk, runny noses, incomplete assignments and undone chores. And second, love knows that God is Lord -- of our finances, marriages, unplanned pregnancies, and our tempers. Love is enduring and steady, and doesn't withhold tenderness in the midst of disappointments.

How is this patience imaginable? *Christ has shown me how to endure.* Before Jesus Christ endured the Cross, He first endured the daily indignities of living with humans. He lived with parents and several siblings in humble circumstances, yet He never sinned - slammed a door, swore, sulked, or screeched. Christ proved that love is patient; Christ showed that love *suffers* a long time. It does not bellow, while throwing the silverware to the floor, "I am not putting up with this a minute longer!"

Love is Kind ... in Word and Deed
Kindness, sadly, is not on my lips when I confront disobedience, disorder or extra chores. But *love* is kind, Paul says. Matthew Henry observes, "The law of kindness is on her lips," referring to the passage in Proverbs 31. The woman who fears God, " ... when she opens her mouth in wisdom ... the teaching of kindness is on her tongue," (Proverbs 31:26). Mom can regulate the racket in her home with the very words that flow from her lips!

Homeschooling moms can wreck more than their academic agendas by lashing children with their tongues. Speaking imprudently, we can destroy trust and succeed only in training disrespectful, angry children. *"A fool does not delight in understanding, but only in revealing his own mind ... A fool's mouth is his ruin, and his lips are the snare of his soul."* Proverbs 18: 2,7

As we guard our lips, stop and "wait long enough for the effect of godly discipline to take root," Mr. Henry counsels. "Love expects to see the kindly effects of patience on him who slights me." The Holy Spirit doesn't badger you when you are under conviction. Sometimes He becomes *very* silent. So, too, love can wait, quietly confident of God's faithfulness. While waiting to see the kindly effects of love, we must get busy!

93

Kind deeds are not always my preference when I face opposition. Nevertheless, "Love seeks to be useful ... seizes and searches for opportunities of doing good," advises our seventeenth century mentor. This recommendation warns against sulking and murmuring, and some of my other favorite responses.

By the way, love rejoices in the children God has entrusted to our care. The fictional June Cleaver never insisted Beaver be just like Wally, nor did she compare either son to other children. Finally, we would do well to remember, cautions Matthew Henry, "Love does not raise tumults or disturbances. Love calms angry passions instead of raising them. Love is not cross nor is it contradictory." *How* we settle problems among our children and between ourselves is fundamental!

Words and Deeds Can Obscure "Love"
Continuing his commentary on Paul's description of love, Matthew Henry says "Love is not unseemly, doing nothing out of time or place, but behaving with courtesy and good will towards all men." Rudeness, seething, pouting or derision come naturally to Adam's offspring, and must not be sanctioned, particularly by our examples -- such as hurling silverware about.

Moreover, Matthew Henry points out that "charity is the enemy of selfishness. It often neglects its own for the sake of others." This is a complete contradiction to this "me-centered" generation's conventional wisdom! You and I do not *deserve* a break today.

Consequently, despite fatigue and disappointment, love is not exasperated. How? "Where the fire of love is kept in, the flames of wrath will not easily kindle, nor long keep burning," writes Matthew Henry. If love reigns in my heart (See Galatians 5:22), then anger cannot rest there. Oh, anger may drop in for a visit -- but

94

if Christ rules, I won't invite it in for a cup of tea and a chat -- I will send anger packing!

Watch Your Thoughts and Your Mouth!

Matthew Henry says, "Charity does not *suspect* evil." What does he mean? He certainly doesn't mean that a loving person is insensible to evil. Rather, he means that love and suspicion are inconsistent. Until we observe sin, we shouldn't assume someone is sinning, even though we know that in the flesh dwells no good thing (See Romans 7:18).

In many situations we cannot "trust in man," including our children (Psalm 118:8). However, a mother or dad can trust God to reveal the facts that expose a need to correct a child. A trusting, open eye is more effective than a suspicious mind. An attitude of trust encourages honesty. An open eye, instructed by Scripture, recognizes weakness or sin. Correcting with an attitude of trust and confidence in God we can help build in our children a regard for what is right and a passion to live rightly.

Also, we must evaluate our words and actions carefully. Truly, "the sins of others [should first] stir compassion," Mr. Henry urges; in words and deeds. Condemnation is not our privilege. The fervent Mother's prayer should cry out "Lord, please help my beloved child who is struggling with besetting sin! Set her, or him, free from the tempter's power."

"Love," Matthew Henry writes, "considers no entertainment in the sins of others ... [and doesn't] expose faults of brothers in public." Don't broadcast your children's failures for the amusement of family and friends. Also, if you have a grievance, tell your child first. If you ask others for prayer, *be discreet*!

Love Beareth All Things

"Charity does not destroy prudence." A loving parent is not insensitive to reality. Clearly, Matthew Henry believes "wisdom may dwell with love and charity be cautious ... Charity is apt to believe well ... if, in spite of this inclination, it cannot believe well, love will yet hope well."

Almost as if he could foresee the demanding days of home education, Matthew Henry chides us by reminding us, "Charity makes the best of everything." Why? Love is not blind; *love believes God*! In whatever our circumstances, we trust God for God keeps His promises, though we fail routinely to observe our end of the bargain. Such love never fails - though our teaching skills fail; though the books and projects fade; though the schooling ends, this love perseveres and triumphs.

May God have mercy and forgive and rectify my sorry representation of Jesus Christ to my children - even today.

ME, An Idol Worshipper?

"[A]nd do not turn aside from any of the words which I command you today, to the right or to the left, to go after other gods to serve them. " Deuteronomy 28:14

Anger is sometimes portrayed humorously and we laugh heartily when we see irascible characters lampooned. However, living with angry people is another matter; as is mastering our own anger! Real-life anger is an emotion that exposes how I think about my self, others, and God.

What is Anger?
The Bible speaks about anger in hundreds of verses, usually admonishing believers against it. Is anger *always* sin? Not invariably. Jesus got mad when He was provoked (Mark 3:5). There is a difference between righteous wrath and anger, and it is easy to identify. Are you willing to look at an emotion that disables Christian parents and cripples their children?

Tom Wenger* suggests some distinctions we should learn to make, to overcome anger and help our children overcome a besetting sin of this generation.

---

* Tom Wenger is an associate pastor of the Severna Park Evangelical Church in Pasadena, Maryland. A graduate of Lancaster Bible College and the Reformed Episcopal Seminary, Tom is a member of the Association of Nouthetic Counselors. He is married to Joanne Wenger and the father of seven children. His remarks taken from the "Anger Workshop," June 6, 1995 at the church.

"Anger," Tom asserts, "is a God-given emotion to help solve problems, not to attack people and create other problems." Hence, Tom continues, "Righteous anger follows when we are offended because someone transgresses the Law of God -- for example lying, murder or dishonoring parents." Tom points out that, "Righteous anger is always accompanied by desire for repentance; righteous anger leads us to pray." Righteous anger does not feel entitled to explode, slam doors, smash walls, or holler, *"I am really fed up with this!"*

However, many insignificant problems of daily living generate anger: causes ranging from misplaced nail clippers, to spilled milk, to rebukes from spouses and Christian friends. But Tom points out these do not necessarily justify anger. Seething, growling, ranting, fuming or glowering, the outward evidence of anger, do not spring from an unselfish concern that God has been offended. No, angry responses commonly spring from a selfish feeling that we are not getting our way.

We do our children no favor by indulging anger -- theirs or ours. "Venting" -- yelling, slamming doors and cursing may temporarily cow a rebellious child into submission, but it will not conform the child to the image of Jesus Christ. Such parental anger only leads to two dead ends. "Children of angry parents," Tom says, "learn to present a front that keeps a lid on things; and to respond to problems of daily living by clamming up or blowing up. If children learn only to control outward appearances, we risk teaching them to become 'socially acceptable idol worshippers' instead of young people whose hearts are right with God," warns Tom. *Idol worshippers?!*

Tom asks us to seriously consider this proposition about anger to see if its fits reality. "The anger that plagues believers and their children is seldom a righteous response to the trampling of God's law, nor does an angry person promote the work of God." Our anger is usually an outward manifestation of an inward passion for worshipping our own personal preferences instead of the true God. Tom argues that anger spews out of a heart full of *idols*.** We blithely excuse pursuing our personal preferences the way Israel excused itself seeking after other gods. Anger erupts when our personal idols get knocked about; or when our children believe their personal idols are under attack.

Inventory Your Throne Room
Do you want to rid yourself of anger and rage (See Colossians 3:8)? Do you know what is on the throne of your heart? Our idols may have less ominous sounding names than Dagon or Molech or Baal, but, Tom reminds us, "they are equally as detestable."

The names of our idols are so much a part of our vernacular that we believe they are part of our nature. Tom points out, "Twentieth century apologists declare man longs for 'security' and 'significance'; for 'self-esteem' and 'approval'." To the contrary, the Bible declares that the chief end of man is to *rejoice in the Lord* no matter the circumstances!

In the inner throne room of your heart, what are you bowing to instead of Jesus Christ - beauty, prominence, security, health, prosperity, perfection? *We can't bow in two directions simultaneously!* Whatever we think about a lot and love the most is an idol, and we all have them - whether it is personal peace, convenience or affluence! Anger explodes - or freezes - when "idols" are knocked about.

**Ed Welsh, *Addictive Behavior*, Baker Books, 1995

Our darling youngsters are also adept at building thrones for their idols, and their angry outbursts can mean their idols are getting knocked about. Do you wonder what the idols of your child's heart may be - popularity, greed, competition? Their anger originates in their hearts and is fed by the choices they seek or encounter. Angry children have hearts that tend to attract and to seek friends with angry hearts, and they feed their angry emotions with violent art and music.

Pray that your children might not sin against God *in their hearts* (Job 1:5). The powerful persistent prayers of parents for their children can successfully attack the "high places" in their hearts. The first altar that must go, however, is located in *our* hearts. Get rid of whatever you have put in Christ's rightful place!

With undivided hearts, we can begin to solve the problems of daily living, and equip our kids to be godly problem solvers instead of angry manipulators. Remember you can't persuasively teach what you haven't learned to practice.

"In moments of calm, talk to your kids," counsels Tom. "Parents derive their authority from God, to represent God. Tell them what God expects of His representatives and their children, and set reasonable behavior expectations. Be consistent with your judgments and be consistent in how you treat different children. Establish and follow a system of reasonable rewards and consequences. *Allow* them to be angry -- but teach them how to deal with anger."

Many angry outbursts in the home happen when children do not obey their parent's instructions. Have our children learned they will get only angry reactions and not firm, godly chastisement? When this happens, we see *we have not taught them how to avoid sin!* (Ephesians 4:25-27). "Children will respond when they know they must," Tom said. "Their response is at the level of requirement." Parents don't do their children any favors by excusing disobedience until we explode in anger and frustration. Therefore we must promptly use external influences to train timely responses in our children. Doing so, we begin to overcome the awfulness of our anger, and avoid exasperating them. Because we live in a world full of sinners, "overcoming anger is never a closed issue, nor does anger submit to quick remedies," Tom reminds.

Help!

Real change happens when we both address our idols and help our kids to understand the root of their anger. Tom asks us to examine *what* is fomenting anger in our home.

"Analyze the problem. Address the problem that is inciting anger, but do not attack the person," even when this sin is infuriating. Judge if "a child is trampling my authority or God's authority," Tom recommends. "If the problem is a sin against God, such as lying, do not tolerate it."

Next consider if "the anger generating problem is an idol of the heart - mine or theirs?" (Who is getting crossed, or whose idol is getting knocked?) Respond according to the severity of the problem. If the problem is a question of manners -- how they dress or cut their hair -- then advise and encourage your child to do what honors God, Tom recommends.

Finally, "decide if the anger-producing problem is simply an irritation like cracking knuckles or tapping a table. Then appeal to them to avoid or cease behavior that disturbs others for the sake of courtesy." Again, act promptly, before the sounds or movement have driven you to distraction. As you pray without ceasing for your

children's hearts to be set on seeking God . . . *believe*
God will give you the powers of persuasion that enable
you to bring glory to *Him!* The earlier we begin working
on anger, the better, Tom urges.

Do you fear too much has happened for you to
recoup? "Too late," you lament. "Not Necessarily," Tom
replies. Remember Paul of Tarsus, the persecutor of the
early Christians? Long after he left the care of his
parents, Paul was transformed from an angry persecutor
to an apostle of Christ by the intervention of Christ
Himself (Acts 9). The Lord can do as much for you and
for your children. So, although you may count much of
your prior life as loss, like Paul resolve to press on that
you may take hold of that for which Christ Jesus took
hold of you! (Philippians 3:12)

PART FOUR

"Body Life"

"And let the peace of Christ rule in your hearts, to which indeed you were called in one body; and be thankful."
Colossians 3:15

Maintaining the Health of the Body:
The Believer's Role

Maintaining the health of our bodies is an American preoccupation. Fitness-conscious individuals devote countless hours, and buckets of sweat to burn fat, tone muscles and purge the impurities from their systems. No one else can exercise or diet for us; it's our decision to get fit and stay fit.

Maintaining the health of the Church requires the same passionate and individual commitment to the Body's well-being. Christ was specific about the health maintenance He expected His family to practice. Yet we often seem more interested seeking "second opinions" or resting by the sidelines, watching as others "work-out."

When The Body Breaks Down

Christians frequently flinch when we observe the inner workings of the Church, hoping an expert or a skilled professional can repair the deviance from the biblical ideal. The cure however, begins with us, one by one - praying and reconciling, restoring the Body to health. James admonished us to confess our faults one to another, *that we may be healed*. The effective prayer of a righteous man can accomplish much (James 5:16). Do you pray for healing, for health in the Body of Christ?

While sin weakens the members in the Body of Christ, and fosters division in the Church, remember its members are related to one another in Christ through faith. His blood atones for and his spirit sanctifies my sister or brother with whom I am fussing.

When we suffer in the Church, because of the Church, it hurts. "Wounds" that disable the Church may begin with a careless remark, or gesture, and multiply out of control as transgressions accumulate. Bloated with hurt, anger, or indignation, the "sore" ruptures, spilling emotions that break friendships in Christ.

What is our response? Do we comply with the prescription Christ was careful to leave with His disciples? (Matthew 5: 23-24; and 18:15-20). Sadly we often do not, walking away, offended and disillusioned. Keeping a record of wrongs, we refuse the steps of reconciliation and the hurt compounds, spreading through the Body, weakening it. How this must grieve the indwelling Holy Spirit. Sadly, the Church often stumbles because grievances are not reconciled according to the prescription of the Great Physician.

How to Restore Health!
Paul carefully prescribed for a young pastor, how to maintain a healthy family (I Timothy 3:1-13). The old apostle explained to avoid "infections," the flock must be very careful how they lived (Ephesians 5:1-21). Knowing the harm that fissures can cause, the Lord Jesus told quarreling believers to reconcile with one another (Matthew 5:23-24; 18:15-21). God prescribes both preventive and curative measures. He expects Christians to apply them both in the Spirit for the health of His church - the Body of Christ.

The Bible carefully explains what Christ expects of church leadership. An elder "must be above reproach, the husband of one wife, temperate, prudent, respectable, hospitable, able to teach, not addicted to wine, or pugnacious, but gentle, uncontentious, free

106

from the love of money . . . He must be one who manages his own household well, keeps his children under control with all dignity . . . but if a man does not know how to manage his own household, how will he take care of the church of God? I Timothy 3:1-5

Do we pray that our leaders are conformed to Christ's requirements? Do we pray for the same standards within the flock? Nowhere in Scripture is the flock somehow excused from conforming to righteousness. Are we praying that both we and our leaders will be above reproach?

The Lord Jesus gave us the ministry of reconciliation, having reconciled us to God by His blood, (II Corinthians 5: 18-21). If God reconciled us to Himself on Christ's behalf, may we continue fights that tear relationships and wreck ministries? He specifically taught us to seek out and restore broken relationships (Matthew 5: 23-24; 18:15-20) gently, and to bear one another's burdens (Galatians 6:1-2).

Maintaining the health of the Body of Christ means risking our spiritual care to "family" members - who themselves may be hurting people, very much in need of our care. Maintaining the health of the Body of Christ is not just a formula for healthy fellowship here on earth, but it is fitting us for living in God's eternal kingdom. God intends all His people to spend eternity with Him (including the believers with whom we currently disagree).

Considering God's purposes for His people, are we doing what we should to maintain the health of the Body? Are we taking His prescriptions and following the health regimen as directed by the Great Physician?

Surely, It Is Not I Rabbi?

Worldly folk define themselves by many standards. These include social or financial stratum, education, race, sex, or ethnic group, political persuasion, religious affiliation, or even the brand of car or computer. Once standards are defined, like-minded people form cliques, consciously or unconsciously. A "clique" is a small, exclusive circle of people; a snobbish or narrow coterie. People grouping together in these circles risk offending both God and man. Such standards have no place in the body of Christ, but too often we see them at work.

You may have experienced pointed instances of unthinking rebuffs -- sadly, teens and adults continue to practice childish rites of exclusion and snub people at times. Scripture records many questionable ways in which we define ourselves, sometimes excluding others. Cliques of believers in Rome and Corinth were stumbling others and distracting them from their common identity in Christ. Paul wrote to the Roman church reminding everyone not to think more highly of himself than he ought; but to think so as to have sound judgment, as God has allotted to each a measure of faith (Romans 12:3). Paul also reprimanded the Corinthian church because cliques had sprung up based on whether one had been taught by Apollos or Paul. Paul said the defining standard is whether one belongs to Christ (1 Corinthians 3:11).

Cliques can distract us from fulfilling Christ's
Great Commission, to make disciples of all nations -- not
just the ones that suit us (Matthew 28:19-20). If we can't
see beyond ourselves and actively love one another in the
church, how can we show the love and glory of Christ to
people outside the church? The habit of staying where we
are comfortable may keep us from welcoming those who
are new to Christ or who are different from us. Worse,
cliquishness robs us of enjoying the rich diversity within
the Body of Christ. Blindly, we stumble and wound our
brothers and sisters. Am I captive to a cliquish
mentality, you ask? Test yourself:

- Am I ill at ease with folks whose skin is
"different" skin, whose hair, clothing, or
testimony is unusual?
- Do I ignore new people, instead of welcoming
them into the Body of Christ which found room
for me?
- Do I feel awkward mingling with different
groups of people in the church, and if so, why?
- Would Christ feel at home in my circle of
Christian friends - or would He feel like
an intruder in private conversations?

Hmmmmm.

A cliquish, exclusive spirit can enter any group --
senior saints, youth groups, ethnic groups, groups that
share a common interest (sports, drama, etc.), groups
defined by marital status, groups fighting present or past
addictions, and many others. True, groups like these
frequently give individual comfort and help, especially
when the larger church seems inaccessible. But such
subgroups must be vigilant lest their focus blur, and they
separate comfort and help from worship of Jesus Christ

and lead the church astray (Hebrews 10:19-25).

How can I avoid cliquish or snobbish behavior? First, I can think about what I would do if I met Jesus in person in the same settings where I meet other people.

- If Jesus dropped in at youth group one night, would I ignore him or brush Him off because I liked my *old* friends better?

- If I sensed Jesus were lonely and pleading for my company, would I beg off visiting because of my *"church" activities*?

- If Jesus were coming to Sunday lunch, would I arrange the meal so I had time to enjoy His company? Would I think ahead and invite some of His other friends?

- If Jesus looked different (poor, old, wounded or, disabled) would I recoil from expressing love and listening to Him?

God can remove the blindness, insensitivity or plain disobedience that betrays Christ and builds barriers between ourselves and others in Christ's body. Let's ask God to show us, now, our self-centeredness or unwillingness to serve and be friendly. Let's ask Him to make us want to turn from what we want, to what He wants; to define us as He wishes and help us stop defining ourselves!   •

Do You Need To Change Your Name?

*"He made Him who knew no sin to be sin on our behalf,
that we might become the righteousness of God in Him.*
2 Corinthians 5:21

Writers of the books of the Bible understood better
than we do how spiritual truths can be instantly and
accurately communicated by our conduct -- the way we
talk, look and act. They knew when people see
Christians they instantly see the Gospel *or* our
misrepresentation of it. What do your children, friends
and neighbors see in you? Is it the "light" of Gospel, *or*
your misrepresentation of it?

Communicating God's "light" doesn't depend
upon word processors, e-mail or satellite dishes
(Matthew 5:14). The world quickly sees whether we are
devoted to Christ, or devoted to self-indulgences while
calling ourselves "Christians." Christ came to give us
new life. Yet, we habitually behave as if Christ came
simply to hold our cloaks while we persist in the muck of
this life until it is finally time to go home! The Lord
Jesus made plain His objective to live a perfect life and
glorify the Father (John 8:46). What is our objective? Is
it the same as Christ's?

"Well, sure I love Jesus, but nobody is perfect,"

111

we mumble, hoping to dodge the issue of obedience to Christ (John 14:15). So what? Many non-Christians revere Christ as some sort of deity or prophet. But, do they *obey* Him? I tell you I respect, honor and *love* my husband! I stood in front of one hundred people and declared my devotion and loyalty to him; *I even took his name!*

If, however, after our wedding I continued living in my own apartment, declining my husband's home unless it suited my fancy, you might doubt my commitment to him? Or, suppose I insisted on preserving an autonomous life - only inviting my husband to join me occasionally. Would you suspect my profession of love? Furthermore, suppose while pursuing my own course, I continued exploiting his name and charged all my debts to *his* account - assuming he'd be pleased to pay because he loves me. How much credence would you give my avowal of esteem and devotion to my husband?

The world rejects the claims of many professing Christians because, like the "wife" I've described, they clearly are not yoked to Jesus Christ (Matthew 11:28-30). These scarcely yoked Christians are trusting a public profession of Christ is sufficient to cover their sins.

It is true we must confess with our mouths that Jesus paid for our salvation; but He paid dearly " *that* we might become the righteousness of God in him." 2 Corinthians. 5:21 "That" means He saved us for *His* own purposes. The good news is redeemed Christians now can freely choose *not* to sin (Proverbs 16:25)! His death on the cross rescued us from sin and death and freed us to become the righteousness of God! Is this the message our lives are broadcasting? Our messages get around.

Word of a cowardly soldier's failure reached the ears of his commander. The well-known story tells that Alexander the Great was irate to learn that one of his soldiers -- also named Alexander -- fled from the enemy. He sent for the spineless soldier, and curtly ordered him to *"Change your conduct, or change your name!"*

Christian if you face Christ tonight, what would He tell you about the use of His name? Openly professing His name while continuing to sin dishonors Christ. Continuing in sin, we perplex non-Christians seeking to know what we believe, and discourage new Christians. What He commands is clear: *"Therefore you are to be perfect, as your heavenly Father is perfect"* (Matthew 5:48). That is Christ's ambition. Is that ours?

"A good name is to be more desired than great riches, favor is better than silver and gold." (Proverbs 22:1) If we value a good name and its favor for ourselves, shouldn't we place an even higher value on the good name of Jesus Christ?

PART FIVE

The Holidays

"And whatever you do in word or deed, do all in the name of the Lord Jesus, giving thanks through Him to the Father." **Colossians 3:17**

God's First "Christmas Gift"

By Doug Smith

Many wise men and women think ahead, and do all their shopping long before Christmas. And, being wiser than any of us, *God decided what he would give us for Christmas long before we ever thought about Him.* (Genesis 3)

The redemption that Christians celebrate at Christmas, *began in the Garden of Eden.* In the garden, Satan--the devil--persuaded Eve to question God's motives for putting the Tree of Knowledge of Good and Evil "off limits" (3:5). Eve, and then Adam, believed Satan--and insulted God--then disobeyed God by eating fruit from the forbidden tree. (3:6)

Immediately, a barrier grew up between husband and wife (3:7); and between the couple and God (3:10). That would have been the end--our situation now--if God hadn't come into the garden prepared with a judgment on Adam and Eve that included mercy as well as justice.

God cursed Satan (3:14), but he did not curse Adam and Eve; rather he chastened them and *set in motion their redemption and ours*:

-God made Satan and the woman hostile to one another -- a valuable protection to Eve and her descendants (3:15).

- God promised that the "seed of the woman"--Jesus Christ--would bruise Satan's head, while Satan would merely bruise Christ's heel (3:14).

So when Jesus told the Jewish ruler Nicodemus to believe in Him and be saved, he wasn't saying anything new; he was restating a promise that was already several thousand years old (John 3:16).

The promise of salvation, given to Adam and Eve, is still valid today--a free gift. The gift is the sacrifice made by Jesus Christ for our sins.

But, like most gifts, you can't have it unless you open it.

Whose Party Is It, Anyway?

Christmas

"And their banquets are accompanied by lyre and harp, by tamborine and flute, and by wine; But they do not pay attention to the deeds of the Lord, nor do they consider the work of His hands. " Isaiah 5:12

The world embraces wholeheartedly the excitement over the anniversary of Jesus Christ's birth, and I am not immune from the thrill of the season. The world's Christmas - a "winter solstice"- revels in plenty of great stuff, in which I also delight. Gifts, lights, even angels, glorious music, laughter, pleasure, good stories, and uncommonly scrumptious food and drink combine to make the season absolutely enchanting.

However, the world's ecumenical commemoration blends creche, angels, and camels, Santa and elves, cartoon characters, Kwanzaa candles and Hanukkah into a confusing montage of symbols. So it is easy to lose sight of the source of the celebration - the birth of Jesus Christ, carefully recorded by the apostles Matthew and Luke.

Reading the accounts of Christ's birth, we quickly discover Scripture does not stipulate most of our Christmas observances. Our Christmas observances spring from a collection of cultures. As the Gospel ignited nation after nation, the church frequently integrated provincial customs into local church practice.

The first calendar reference to December 25 is on a Roman one in 336 A.D., * and the Roman

---

*   *The World Book Encyclopedia*, 1989, vol. 3, pp. 528-537.

Empire was the first nation to adopt Christianity as the state religion in 330-ish A.D. Plenty of interesting customs that would have been familiar to former pagans, have survived to become what we consider "our traditions." For example, preparing special foods, decorating our homes with greenery, and singing and giving gifts are traditions rooted firmly in the pagan past. We have been enjoying our traditions for such a long time, and in so many nations, no wonder we forget *the person* whose birthday the Church commemorates on December 25!

Did *you* forget His "birthday party," because you are so wrapped up with "Christmas?" I am ashamed to admit that the Lord Jesus' name is hardly ever the first name on my Christmas list. Honestly, I don't plan for His birthday as carefully as I do our children's parties or my husband's. Nor do I spend much time wondering how Christ would enjoy His birthday if He spent it at our house this year. If He would drop by on the morning of the twenty-fifth, would He know the holiday festivities were to honor Him? (How would my loved ones or neighbors *know*?) Have I even thought about a present for the guest of honor?

Maybe like me you need to untangle yourself from the revelry, and appropriate time to consider Him whom we seek to honor, and why we honor Him. As the frenzy of holiday preparations and commotion converge, we may forget, like Israel, who our God is. As the prophet Isaiah warned Israel, his words pointedly remind us: the world's way of keeping Christmas can so permeate our observance, *we forget God*, what He has done for us through Christ, and what His wants for us. *"And their banquets are accompanied by lyre and harp, by tamborine and flute, and by wine; But they do not pay attention to the deeds of the Lord, nor do they consider*

120

the work of His hands" Isaiah 5:12

Before you generate more Christmas activities, trace the promises of Christmas in the Old Testament - there are many - and how God fulfilled them in Christ. He isn't frozen in time as a newborn in a stable in Bethlehem. He is alive, and seated at the right hand of God (Hebrews 10:12).

If you are content to glance quickly at the sweet newborn sleeping soundly, remember He grew into the man who appeared suddenly at the Temple, cleansing it with a whip. If you try to imagine His tiny fingers curling perhaps around Mary's finger, remember one day decades later, His hand would be contorted in agony, nailed to the cross on your behalf. If you see in your mind's eye, the Baby's gentle breathing in and out, remember He rose from the dead to give eternal life to those who trust Him. That precious babe is the One who is preparing a place especially designed for you, and He is coming back to escort you home.

Roaring into the Christmas season spiritually unprepared, anticipating something "magical" will happen to revitalize your spirit, can prove as disappointing as roaring up on any Sunday expecting a "high" from a sermon and a choir. Stop right now for a moment and consider Christ whom we say we wish to honor. Deliberately prepare yourself and your family to enjoy Christ's birthday - not as the world does, by wearing yourself out with "tradition," but by seeking Him in His word by prayer. The *joy* of the season *will* follow! Not as the world understands it, but as He gives it.

The Christmas celebration will be enriched if we give the Christ Child the gift of our time and attention. Our family can make a real choice about priorities this Holiday. How about yours?

Olives Can Be Hazardous to Your Health
Happy New Year!

Over the Christmas holidays I am always thirsty,
perhaps because I eat more sweets than normal and
probably because I eat many more salty foods than I am
accustomed to eating. Without fail, during the holidays I
never encounter an inedible piece of fudge or an
unappetizing olive. But all these normally forbidden
goodies make me thirsty!

Have the holidays made you thirsty for God?
When the delights of the season begin to fade as you put
away the decorations and accouterments of Christmas, do
you detect a spiritual dryness in your heart? Does your
soul pant after the Living God, the way you hanker for
cool water when arising in the morning? (Psalm 42:1).

The holiday parties and presents, food and
frippery, the concerts, cinema and ballets rarely
nourish, do they? Nor do any of our amusements fortify
us for the rigors of returning to our homeschool duties
and their companion domestic responsibilities. Our
holiday diversions are simply that - distractions, but
often at the expense of spiritual refreshment that sustains.

Having feasted on the delights of the season, I
often awake, parched and despairing, worried that God
might reject me. Thirsty and sleepless and like the
psalmist I begin to bemoan my circumstances. Fearing
failure - my own, my husband's, and my children's - I
sigh because of the tasks at hand (Psalm 42:9).
Are you with me?

Our souls despair because we are hoping in things other than God for our relief. A constant snare for Christians, is seeking relief in diversions instead of simply resting in His presence (Psalm 42:5).

We see the consequence of misplaced hope clearly on the twenty-sixth of December. The stores that only 48 hours before heralded the delights of the season, now overflow with aggravated shoppers. However, now they are busily returning gifts or seeking "bargains" on the desires of their hearts that weren't wrapped under the tree, or were the wrong size and color.

How do you find Christ in the aftermath of the holidays, if you are thirsty? How will you find Him now, especially if you first lost sight of Him at the Mall? Where can you find Him after the creche is packed away? He is as near as your water tap, but nearer. He isn't hiding and dodging you, the way you and I may sometimes dodge and hide from Him.

He is the friend who is closer than a brother, so don't postpone prayer and fellowship with Him. He has a great deal on His mind - don't let your Bible stay tucked under the remaining debris of the holiday! There is a grand invitation in those pages:

"Ho, Everyone who thirsts, come to the waters; And you who have no money come, buy and eat ... without money and without cost. " Isaiah 55:1

He has never failed me so, *why* do I fret that He will reject my husband and me, and abandon my children? I *can* rejoice in His Word, which tells me my God has plans for each of us, plans for our welfare and not our calamity (Jeremiah 29:11)! My hope is wrapped up, new each morning - not just on the twenty-fifth of December.

Come - listen - *delight yourself in abundance*. Listen, that you may *live*!

123

Has There Ever *Been* Such A Morning?
Easter

"I am the resurrection and the life; he who believes in Me shall live even if he dies, and everyone who lives and believes in Me shall never die. Do you believe this?"
John 11:25-26

Death is calling more frequently, snapping what always felt like unbreakable bonds to dear friends and family. The initial trauma of beholding the dead body of a familiar family member or fond acquaintance has subsided. Appearing to sleep, each is plainly the unfeeling, empty shell of someone who once was important to me. Whatever it was that defined the person who stirred my love and loyalty is gone. Even my memories of the person, (which some folks trust to confer "immortality"), will fade and when I die, they will vanish. Once buried each body remains in the grave. This particularly besets my soul with sorrow and regret.

The Lord Jesus Christ's body was as dead as those I've helped to bury. Whatever it was that made Him the man who stirred the hearts of the first century Jews and Gentiles, departed when He said, "it is finished," and gave up His spirit (John 19:30). However Jesus did not stay buried. This truth is the hope of my daily life.

I can understand "crucifixion"; this is how Romans executed criminals on a cross. I wonder at thesuffering and death of Jesus Christ, on my behalf. However, His resurrection is beyond my comprehension.

Nothing in my physical life's experience remotely corresponds to the mystery and power that brought Christ Jesus again from the dead. No, I have had no experience that revealed a perfectly restored physical human body, resurrected from death. A dead body again empowered and flawlessly functioning. Yet Jesus Christ walked out of the tomb on the third day, according to the Scripture, sound, undamaged and intact, though bearing the marks of His crucifixion in His body.

Angels didn't carry Him out of the tomb on a stretcher, nor did the Lord Jesus hobble out, wincing in pain. Roman spikes pounded through a man's foot would be enough to mangle permanently any bones - yet He required no crutches. The weight of His body hanging on the Cross for six hours stretched every muscle, and pulled every bone from its socket - yet He stood erect. The thrust of Roman spear punctured His heart and perhaps lungs, spilling water and blood - yet He breathed. He will never again die, so His grave clothes were folded and put aside. Because He walked out of that tomb, I know the power available to me and to every believer who confesses that Jesus Christ is Lord and believes in their heart that God raised Him from the dead. (Romans 10:9-10)

So, when my pastor asked in his sermon, "Do you believe that Jesus Christ is not dead?", his question jolted me! I know what death looks like and Jesus Christ is not dead. The reminder of the central joyous doctrine of the Christian faith is a powerful tonic. Staggering out from winter's cave, recovering from bugs, academic pressures, and family worries, to confront the inescapable fact, *Jesus Christ is not dead*, surpasses the sparkle of spring sunshine and fragrant breezes.

However the pastor's query continues to stir up my thoughts. Jesus Christ's human life affected thousands of people in a tiny, obscure part of the Roman Empire; but His resurrected life changed the course of history for every human life before and after the event - for all eternity. What *does* it mean to me, apart from the Easter festivities, that Jesus Christ is not dead, but alive and His spirit is living in me? How does the resurrection alter my life?

Both King David, living almost a thousand years before Christ, and the fisherman Peter, Christ's contemporary, were changed men because of the resurrection - one anticipating it, the other looking back to it. (Psalms 16:8-11; Acts 2:27). David wrote, and later Peter preached his words:

"I was always beholding the Lord in my presence. For He is at my right hand that I might not be shaken. Therefore, my heart was glad and my tongue exalted. Moreover my flesh also will abide in hope. Because thou will not abandon my soul to Hades, nor allow Thy Holy One to undergo decay. Thou hast made known to me the ways of life; Thou wilt make me full of gladness with thy presence. " Acts 2:27

David described the Lord "always at my right hand." I write with my right hand, I work with it, and that is where He is - *that I might not be shaken.* Because He knows my future, what I will experience, *He will not abandon me.* He shows me from His Word, through the power of His Holy Spirit *the ways of life!* Moreover, because He, the Holy One, did not undergo decay, *my flesh will abide in hope!* What I have never seen with my physical eye, I have experienced daily. What I cannot touch with my hand, I rely upon with all my heart. What I cannot fathom, sustains me.

126

So what is my point, as my son is fond of asking. The power that resurrected Christ from death is a free gift to those who ask for it. My purpose is best described by a Pharisee who finally saw the light, the apostle Paul. As Paul prayed for the Ephesians, I am praying for those who are my friends and family:

"... that the eyes of your heart may be enlightened in order that you may know the hope to which he has called you, the riches of his glorious inheritance in the saints, and his incomparably great power for us who believe. That power is like the working of his mighty strength, which He exerted in Christ when he raised him from the dead ... " (Ephesians 1:18-20 N.I.V)

Hallelujah! Christ is Risen!
Has there ever been such a Morning?

Postscript

In laying out the design of our book on the computer, I forgot to insert one little word -- an instruction that told the printer how to print the pages. Unaware of my error, I worked for hours importing the text into a publishing program.

Sighing with relief, I watched the printer expecting crisp, clean copy. However, the printer refused to produce the pages I intended! Stunned, I watched as the printer spit out a corrupted copy of our manuscript. Frantic, I knew I had made an instruction error. *Back to the instruction manual!*

Starting over, I quickly found the missing word . *One little word*, left out of a simple set of instructions, and an afternoon's work was scrambled! Chastened, I reread the manual, solving the problem plus I discovered some tips to simplify my work.

I am not recounting this vexation to gain your sympathy. Through this minor printing disaster the Lord showed me how omitting or adding even small words - through carelessness or ignorance -- can distort our most ambitious work for Him.

If one missing word can garble the message of an entire book, how will negligent or pompous words garble the message of our homeschool plans? We hope we have not overlooked or added any words telling you what we have learned.

We have learned *Grace* and *Mercy* in our experiences. We are learning from the essential duo: *Humility and Gratitude* - which is the underpinning of *Kindness and Self-Control*. We continue to learn *Repentance*, without which we could not infuse *Patience* into all we do and say. In our expectations, we have learned not to neglect *Faith* and *Joy*. Nor to forget to insert *Hope and Joy in the Lord* into all our "operating instructions!"

Thanks for reading our book. We hope we have encouraged you to seek God and His direction for you home education program. If we did leave out some words, maybe the Lord will give you a message to communicate. Ask Him.

And we would love to hear from you!

128